PRAISE FOR POEMCITY

"I look forward to bringing in spring with poems . . . to
the creativity and imagination of hundreds of people
making our community a more joyful, compassionate and
welcoming place."

—Scudder Parker, Middlesex

"PoemCity is a wonderful event offering a chance for poets
living in Vermont, published and not, to appear side by
side on window fronts in Montpelier."

—Deb Franzoni, Castleton

"The Kellogg-Hubbard Library has . . . welcomed LGBTQ
poets into Montpelier's annual Poem City celebration."

—Linda Quinlan, Montpelier

"I love participating in the events at PoemCity, listening to
my fellow Vermont poets."

—Geza Tatrallyay, Barnard

"I am looking forward to a new flood of poems this coming
April, just when we need them most."

—Florence McCloud, South Burlington

"PoemCity is like a garden in mid winter, flowers breaking
through the snow. I am proud to have seen some of those
blooms."

—Philip Coleman, South Burlington

"PoemCity is a warm, inclusive community, and having
been included in it a couple of times is a validation and a
welcome."

—*Ann Cooper, Middlebury*

"Writing poems every year . . . together with my parents
is one of my most precious memories . . . Thank you
for creating this wonderful opportunity for family
togetherness."

—*Susan Chickering, East Montpelier*

"Retired journalist, longtime Montpelier resident, looking
forward to the amazing range of creativity from our
community put on display each April."

—*Dave Gram, Montpelier*

"This PoemCity, I am looking forward to reading the
poems. Perhaps I will take a friend after school . . . reading
as many poems as possible. I look forward to seeing those
tell-tale white papers, with the little blue logo in the corner,
dotting the storefronts this year."

—*Rachel Brassard, 7th grader, Main Street Middle School, Montpelier*

"As a poet, I am inspired by the world and my place within
it, and I believe poetry is an artform that is inextricable
from everyday existence, a tool and mode of personal
expression that creates and strengthens relations and
understanding between all things. I am naturally looking
forward to encountering other local poets and enjoying
their work in interesting places."

—*Deven Valliere, Sharon*

"Seeing our downtown windows full of poems throughout the month of April is a real delight for the eyes and the mind and I'm so grateful for the time I've spent moving from street to street taking in poems in the springtime air."

—*Jack Markoski, Montpelier*

"I look forward to PoemCity every year! So many friends have been included over the years and I love how it integrates poetry into the everyday. I want to get a gigantic burrito at Mad Taco and wander the streets reading people's poems."

—*Meg Reynolds, Burlington*

"I love walking through the springtime streets reading poems papering over the windows. The poetry is as changeable as the weather in April."

—*Alice Christian, Colchester*

"I really put a lot of work into this poem and I hope you like it. I'm looking forward to this PoemCity because I am really connected to lots of different types of poetry and I'm excited to see lots of unique and new types of poems."

—*Lydia M. Bearsch, age 10, Main Street Middle School, Montpelier*

"I'm most looking forward to my lunch break walks and walks to work. I'll leave the house earlier just to fill my mornings with poetry."

—*Poa Mutino, Montpelier*

"I love the amazing variety and wealth of poetry bursting
out in Montpelier in April. Who knew there were so many
poets among us?"

—Susan Reid, Montpelier

"PoemCity is a feast that I like to savor, digesting some new
poems and meeting new poetic voices. It's always a treat!"

—Cynthia Liepmann, Middlesex

"I am looking forward to poems blooming in windows as
spring flowers."

—Simon Walsh, Brattleboro

"I look forward to reveling in poetry with Montpelier, the
city where I first began writing poems, where my children
played and learned what community and creativity mean,
where so many of my friendships budded and took root,
where the language of connection has a home."

—Judith Chalmer, Burlington

"Poems are like doors. They transport us. They also bring
us home. Grateful for this happening each year!"

—Aylie Baker, Shelburne

POEMCITY ANTHOLOGY: 2023

Poem City Anthology

• 2023 •

Montpelier, Vermont

First edition: April 2023

ISBN: 978-1-57869-137-1

Library of Congress Control Number: 2023933587

Published by Rootstock Publishing
an imprint of Ziggy Media LLC
32 Main Street #165, Montpelier, VT 05602
info@rootstockpublishing.com
www.rootstockpublishing.com

Compiled by The Kellogg-Hubbard Library
135 Main Street, Montpelier, VT 05502
info@kellogghubbard.org
www.kellogghubbard.org

Designed by Dana Dwinell-Yardley: ddydesign.com.

Cover art by Amanda Weisenfeld, "Fox Contemplates Rabbit as God,"
wet felted wool and hand embroidery, 18'' round ©2022,
photographed by Shanon Casey-King.

Printed in the USA.

CONTENTS

Introduction

Welcome to PoemCity, the Kellogg-Hubbard Library's annual celebration of National Poetry Month in April. For fourteen years, we have hosted dozens of poetry readings and events and turned the windows of downtown businesses in Montpelier, Vermont, into a walkable anthology of poetry by Vermonters. We stop and read the poems of our neighbors and friends while we pick up a coffee, shop, bank, and countless other everyday tasks.

For the first time, we are collecting the poems into this volume, our first printed and bound anthology. If you weren't able to make it to the smallest capital city in the U.S. with the biggest celebration of National Poetry Month, this is your chance to read the work of Vermonters from all corners of the state and from a wide range of experience: for some, this is their first poem; for others, their hundredth.

Thank you for joining us in celebrating poetry.

ACKNOWLEDGMENTS

The Kellogg-Hubbard Library would like to thank the following individuals for their help with this anthology: Dana Dwinell-Yardley, Marisa Keller, Samantha Kolber, Michelle Singer, and Mary Rose Dougherty.

Special thanks to Rachel Senechal and Phayvanh Luekhamhan for creating PoemCity, formally PoetryALIVE!, fourteen years ago. Many volunteers over the years have made PoemCity possible, as well as our community partners and downtown Montpelier business owners—our heartfelt thanks go to them. Generous support from National Life Group, Vermont Humanities, and the Hunger Mountain Coop has made PoemCity thrive.

Another special thanks to Shanon Casey-King and Amanda Weisenfeld for the cover art, which Amanda created as an artistic response to Shanon's poem on page 50. "Fox Contemplates Rabbit as God" is a poem in two parts: one part written, one part visual. It is a collaboration between a poet and felt artist who both engage in a lifelong fascination with myths, fairy tales, and the animal kin that share these landscapes with us.

Finally, thank you to all the poets and readers. The following poems have been printed with permission.

Poems

The Pray-ers

These are the honey makers
The maple sap tappers
The pollen gatherers
The elixirs healing the future
from the spirits of the past
Unleashing beasts
who make right the wrongs
The saviors of the waters
The elders of the vineyards
Turning failing limbs to wings
Blacksmiths who shape
hard metals into words
Uncoiling spells to rest on winds
and spiral to the sky
These are the doers, the shakers, the spinners
The unripe berries who will delight our tongues
who speak the truth before it is so
and unjam the rivers to free the flow
They are the fish that run upwards
then come down to feed the people
when the best of times are beaten.

—*Buffy Aakaash, Marshfield*

a version of this poem was previously published in *New Feathers Anthology,*
Summer 2022

Third Grade, February 12th, 2020

Our children gather their tools of expression: glitter glue,
paper lace and small-handed scissors, multicolored,
multifaceted layers of construction paper, pepperminty paste,
magic markers that smell of froot loops, grape soda, root beer . . .

and they set to work exploring the depths of their love.
The symmetrical, precision-folded hearts of the art-girls
with sparkles and glue sticks. Traced or folded, wingéd perfection
produced in contrast with the boys' dopey lopsidedness

their freehand lobes of lub-dub lub-dub lub-dub.
Symbols of so much paired human history: eyes, lips, lobes,
our even breathing, in and out . . . We're manufacturing hearts
by the hundreds: beautiful, crooked, broken and perfect.

Our elementary school valentine factory impassioned . . .
for a day and a half, where love's too-much-glue can be easily fixed
with too-much-glitter. Full of unicorns and cupidry, cards ringed
with rainbow stripes, polka-dotted with black magic marker.

Some signed, loopily, *i love you* with a heart-dotted *i*,
origami swans crosshatched in XXs, rhinos inscribed with OOs,
slid into clean white envelopes, and licked closed.
We move down the democratic list of the lovable,
all the checkmarks checked, every envelope with a home.

—*Rick Agran, Worcester*

On a Cloud

On a cloud, on a cloud I find myself floating—
above me the heavens below me the earth—
On a cloud, on a cloud It's where I want to stay—
floating over the world, spreading harmony—
On a cloud, On a cloud it's where I belong—
time disappears when I'm playing a song—
On a cloud, On a cloud with a harp in my hand—
plucking a tune just so absent of beginning and end—
When I finally hang up my hat standing at those pearly gates—
What use is Mammon there?
the music remains but money's value's in flames—
save the souls who had some to share—
I'm on this side still praying my bucket gets filled—
with more than just the air—
On a cloud, On a cloud, on the sidewalk downtown—
a smile's worth more than gold—
my happiness and joy can't be destroyed—
by those who wish I was not—
just drifting along playing an infinite tune—
all about Peace Light AND Love . . .

—*Glow Alexander, Montpelier*

The Old Maples

The old maples down the road
have succumbed to weather
and wind. Yesterday, a bonfire
in the clearing.

Now, a gaping hole of ash
and tire tracks. Trunks
lopped off at the ground,
a sickness of stumps.

It was the most beautiful
road in town, the road
that traveled along the sheep farm,
those maples like sentinels.

A canopy forming
in spring with leafy boughs
meeting and touching across
New England sky.

To drive this road now
is to lament the passage of days.
The steady, sure havoc.

—*Shari Altman, Hartland*

On a morning such as this

On a morning such as this,
The sun paints the frosty vestments of the hayfields
With dances of gold.

The ice on the pond is eggshell-delicate,
And beneath,
The flames of summer sigh their contented dreams.

The long, wise, shadows of the trees
Reach their deep fingers into my heart,
And whisper secrets
Of something solemn, and dark, and utterly wholesome.

On a morning such as this,
Prayer is as simple as breath;
And my love is held immaculate
By the silence of the Earth.

—Eyal Amiel, Morrisville

Iris

Time was when, upon a death,
 all useful things were gladly taken,
 threads, needles, pans, spoons.
What was in places worn might make a patch.
A chipped dish might in another kitchen
 house a plant, some parsley or fragrant rosemary.
From drawers the clan would sort the photographs,
 chat over memories and tea.
Granddaughters would leave with small collections.
A seasoned spoon in a new kitchen
 would stir the batter from an old recipe.

Iris gone, her shadow lies lifeless
 in the cold bungalow. No clan here.
Now the agent ousts the few antiques of value,
 naming them in pounds sterling.
His two lads drag what's left out the door
 and heap it on the lawn,
 coats, gloves, dishes, books.
Photo albums splay open on the wet grass,
 and the rain comes down.

—*Ina Anderson, South Royalton*
from *Journey into Space*, 2017

City Rain

Downpouring rain
waits for no one:
slides, trees to gutters,
flows, roofs to streets

moves, waves crossing itself.
Purifies the urban ground,
washing the grit, flushing the curbs
nourishing, cleansing
asphalt and landscape together.

Rain came today
even the dog hid his nose in his paws
as thunder sounded "kegs rolling across the sky."

My day alone—but not alone

Thunderous calls reached me
begging for attention, scolding, pleading,
threatening, refusing silence

The wings of the chair curled to me

The storm moved on.

—*Juliana Collins Anderson, Williston*
a version of this poem was previously published in *Morning in the World*, 2017

Sunday

I pile all the blankets in the hamper, wake
   soft puffs of dust
from their hibernation under the bed.

 I pour detergent into the MaxoWasher
at the Launderama to
rid us of the stains from the dead of winter.

 I fold underwear in awkward intimacy
   with the people beside me
    fingertips savoring the crisp clean.

Hoping this is what saves us:
sharing the laundromat table and the breeze
from the door propped
open

—Cara M.L. Arduengo, Barre

Snow Writing

You carved a fresh trail through 16 new inches,
winding past the nude ash, maple, black cherry—
old friends we are just matching names to
   on sight
this intimate winter.

You did it for yourself, you may say,
for exercise, a boon to the few neighbors
who also like hiking loops,
climbing up the ridge,
under hemlock canopy where deer bed,
and down the sloping ledge.

But I can read snow writing,
recognize the long slow strokes
of my beloved
in the blue-shadowed message
etched in crystal
between the drifts:

"Come with me, sweetheart."

—Barb Asen, Montpelier

Watermelon

I think of sweetness
and the sharing of it
on a humid morning
in August, cricket call
and crow song, sitting
on a rain-soaked porch
with women who know
bitter and sweet,
know how to tell it,
laugh too, some of us
who've nearly died,
no guarantee that
every day is sweet,
but this morning
we are tasting it.

—S. Atwood, East Montpelier

Adamant Spring

Turkeys scratch, hunger led
still sharp, Winter's edge,
where frost yet clings, in the face of coming Spring
Sun days, trees pulse with sap
icy winds end that;
swirling squalls, freezing cold
reigning season, bold
Winter rages, violent bursts, defiant
Tireless sun adamant,
Winter, worn, relents;
gritty wet, grainy snow
muddy patches show
at last warmth sustained; emerging shoots, ground gained
Turkeys scratch, hunger led
Spring's sprung; they'll be fed

—*D. Slayton Avery, Woodbury*
previously published online, 2021

The Sun

The sun will warm my cheeks
with its warm embrace
and gentle care.
It will wake the weary world,
it will melt the forbidding snow,
and call me outside,
to see the flowers rise
and just in case,
it will keep me there
with the breeze around it twirled.

—Alice B., age 11, Montpelier

Centrifugal Force

Spin
a metal pail of water
over your head

feel
the pail
speed up.
it is now spinning

you.

then,
go faster
f a s t e r
until, you get so dizzy
you fall down
right off the dock, that creaks
moans, sighs
and into the shallow water
and it's

warm
and you're soaked and laughing
and the pail is floating serenely away
already a memory
bobbing away
on the waves.

—Phoebe Bakeman, age 13, Montpelier

Redirection

This afternoon when asked to clean up her snack
four-year-old Lara bursts out—
But a pig kissed a human!

Crumbled cookies give way to peals of laughter
and a hailstorm of kisses tumble over the tables
        pigs kissing birds
            birds kissing bats
                bats kissing butts
                    kissing cows kissing moos kissing
    milk kissing moons
                kissing suns
                kissing sky
                    kissing trees kissing trees
                kissing—

                    As he mouths the words
                        the young boy's eyes
                        turn glassy and distant
                as though suddenly catching sight
                            of his home planet
                    cresting some far-off horizon.

—*Air*
        he says. And we
all look around
            startled.

Air kisses Air

—*Aylie Baker, Shelburne*

On Our Dirt Road

A hay-crammed pickup truck,
bales stuck out each side,
bounces toward me
and my dog. The driver lifts
four fingers as he passes,
thumb still hooked around
the steering wheel, which is more
than the two fingers I raise,
or the index finger some people
offer, which beats out
the arched eyebrow.

One man extends his arm
each time someone drives by
while he's outside working,
rotates his hand backwards
about forty-five degrees,
and, continuing his business,
turns his back to you
because no one wants to seem too friendly
or unfriendly on our dirt road.

—*Charles Barasch, Plainfield*
from *Home Movie*, 2022

Limerick

I went skiing at Bolton
My skiis turned molton
They started to glow
They melted the snow
And I fell into a great big hole
Nobody was sad
so I felt real bad
And I ran back home to Dad

—Skyler Barnard, age 11, Montpelier

shadow

what is a shadow
but proof that light obstructed
nevertheless shines

—Bettie Barnes, South Burlington

Homing

Each return
begins in tree sap, then coltsfoot

the fertile valleys,
the spaces between vertebrae,
they extend with the shadows
of quickening clouds

the clear cold fades
for a cyclical leap,
enough rain to refresh
the shapes of the spine,
the greening fields

The striped maple leaves are not opaque
sun still filters,
wind dances their forms,
humid in the interplay

meet the rise and
fall of the ledge,
where treetops reach out
to roots that cradle the body

—Julia Barstow, East Montpelier

Life, Death, and all that.

Life
Bright, Free
Laughing, Crying, Freeing
Lydia, Eme . . . Cemeteries, Coffins
Nothing, Ending, Dying
Sad, Dark
Death

—Lydia M. Bearsch, age 10, Montpelier

Years Before We Said Hello: A Villanelle

Two trees formed a V
There I placed my heart
Cradled thus I could see

Years before hello said we
Hoping for a new start
Two trees formed a V

I ponder what matters to me
Have I done my part?
Cradled thus I could see

Am I asking too much of eternity?
With yearnings to impart
Two trees formed a V

Yet there I gaze decidedly
Upon my healing heart
Cradled thus I could see

I am calling you to me
For us a course love will chart
Two trees formed a V
Cradled thus I could see

—Jean Elizabeth Beatson, Jericho

Eternal Love

The Sea claws at the Shore,
Saying, "More . . . give me more!"

The Shore cleaves to the Sea,
Says, "I'm yours . . . take all of me!"

—Kim Allen Bent, Montpelier

letter to lake pitawbagok*

in my unseasoned hands
I cradled ancient rocks
found   in plain view

on shore   white scratchings
of snail shell on shale
glacial stories ciphered
by those long dead.

was I expecting life
would be like that—

a clean etching
on a dark surface
found at the right
moment lakeside

no nights of drowning
in disbelief   no drought?

I lie on my back
in your water
while waves lap
a familiar carillon

and I am born
once more in wonder

as the last star
sinks skyward
at dawn

—anne bergeron, West Corinth
**the Abenaki name for Lake Champlain, "the waters between"*
 a version of this poem was previously published in *Blueline Magazine*, 2021

Poem Beginning with the Last Lines
of a Failed Poem

for Nina Riggs

You reached out to me for balance
even though we weren't speaking
and a minute later I had to do the same

or else this random bowl of chance
we share is cracked and leaking
all over a threadbare carpet your name

has slipped under, along with analog
words like *love peace joy* and *kindness*—
offered up into fraught silence then swept

by the soulless, fracked from their catalog
of profitable veins mined in blindness
and deafness. At the time, all that kept

us sane and resilient was reliance
on other perspectives, another unsure
hand to steady the lens of compliance

and shift the focus of our defiance
from an unseen horizon we endure
looming out there on the edge of darkness

to the crumbs beneath a thinning carpet
each big enough to satisfy a mouse or wren:
a walk in the woods, a loaf of fresh bread,

an unfinished watercolor, the starlit
gravity that pulls us to bed, some spot-on
unfiltered thing a small child just said.

—Partridge Boswell, Woodstock
previously published in *Hunger Mountain Review,* Spring 2023

Newborn in Spring

I dreamed of this day
Sitting on the porch with you in my arms
Baby
Listening to the birds chirp—feeling the spring breeze—
    watching the flowers grow pink purple yellow red—
    lavender lilacs busting from the bush—from our
    rocking chair perch
Baby
Sun shining down and clouds rolling lazily—wisps of
    fluffy seeds floating through the air—the sweet sultry
    heaviness of lust filled pollen settled on the face and body
    and ground and everywhere its weight bringing us back
Down
To earth
Baby
The only thing I hadn't accounted for—the sound of the
    train's horn blaring its arrival in the distance
Having just rolled through Vermont's sloping hills it
    sounds its stop in the river valley of Montpelier—before
    making its way North to
Last stop—
St. Albans City
Or South to—
Last stop—
Destination unknown.
That part I didn't account for—
The dream Come to life
Baby

—Abigail O. Bower, Montpelier

Rochester Gap

Spring light
slides through the late afternoon
endless screens of trees.

Glimpses pine needle carpet
now glows with early spring sun
penetrates the sleeping soil.

Vibrant hues of lime, seafoam, fern
emerge from barren branches, brown and gray
step up the hillside to swallow stubborn snow patches.

In the embrace of wild mountains
trees join long arms above
low bundled buds bursting to life.

Cold waters race in unfettered flows
with resounding ripples that remember
ancient awakenings in lakes and ponds.

Their ride continues
to the sea where all life began
waves to the whales from the waterfall.

They seek the sandy shore
where the sharp shiny brine
greets every last stream.

—*Jo Bower, East Montpelier*

A Heavy Sun

Every morning a heavy sun
wanders west like the troubles
of a country song,
sweet like a hat
without any money
or keys to a life
without encumbrance.

Reflecting on the corduroy
fabric of her days, she pulls at
the modest blue collar that follows
the portals of her breathing.
Persistently submerged in the task
of rubbing between the ironies
of her welcome like a prayer.

Go into the fields
strain in the mud and the muck.
Do that to be done, again and again.
Her song harnesses her to a shape
that satisfies the deep and abiding.
Crying for water and work that is real,
she reaps a harvest that asks only for more.

—*Scott Boyd, Stowe*

Peanut Butter Fudge

Anticipation excites as yet another Christmas explodes
with enough sweets to fill a Halloween pillow case!

"We hope Grandma makes her divine Peanut Butter
Fudge this year," is the vibe I'm getting. The expressions
will be subtle, the faces not a grin, are they pretending
not to like it, only Grandma knows what really lies within!

It will be fabulous! Sweet, decadent, creamy, with a
Marshmallow Fluff attitude! Light, airy, cloud like, an
angel with Peanut Butter Wings floating on a puff of
wispy white feathers.

Smothered in love with its spectrum of textures and
desire, my creation for a lasting memory.

"Grandma's Peanut Butter Fudge!"

—Donna Bramley, South Burlington

The remnants of a dream

Where do our minds go when we sleep?

We feel untethered, unbound
No chain to tie us, no anchor to ground us here.

And yet, we are not free.
Something, still, keeps us here.
Maybe it is the hope of a new dawn,
Maybe it is the knowledge of the sun rising,
The security that it will be there,
Day after day,
Until long after we've gone.

—Rachel Brassard, age 13, Montpelier

The Fox Nobody Knows

*"The only native fox in New England, the gray fox is the fox nobody knows, and fewer
people see. A tree climber. An eater of melon and mice, squirrels, frogs, and snakes,
with a taste for carrion."*

*—Naturalist Ted Levin as quoted in Daybreak, accompanied by a clip from Erin
Donahue's trail cam*

Night camera's monotone
captures gray fox
alerted by scent or sound
to stuffed figure frozen on snow
each hair tip aglow
eyes molten silver moons

head swivels left to right
the elusive one
thaws to real
dainty legs trot over snow
last glimpse lush tail
the fox nobody knows
and fewer people see

and if my soul too
slips into the wild
lurks among the shadows
pauses with moon-pooled eyes
what is it that the watcher sees
am I predator
or prey?

—Beverly Breen, Thetford Center

ghost prayer

for now.
let me just say this: when you   dear girl
discover the door at the back of your mind,
the one without a bell the one without a lock
the one draped with rosaries   made of words
smoking from the friction
of gendered dreams
go ahead   walk through it.

all the women in our line
while folding sheets
or slicing meat
while reeling in childbirth
or the shuttling of sex,
          have all been weaving   an amulet
that you might be set to fire
and not burn:

yarn of an unraveled baby's blanket,
dirt from a grave speckled with mica,
the ten moons of your mother's hand,
eyelash of a doe, a window   called hunger,
bead of sweat,   whimper of   prayer—
          the cold clay of courage.

it's ok to go away for a while
          and to (please)   come back

—*Bethany Breitland, Charlotte*
from *Fire Index*, April 2023

Bless This Ordinary Life

Bless this ordinary life—
the dishes stacked in the sink,
the laundry waiting to be folded,
the coffee cool enough to drink . . .

Bless these, our ordinary lives
full of peanut butter, shopping carts,
full of trees leafing out into canopies,
bushes buzzing with the eager bees.

Bless the blessed calm which
at any moment may be ripped away
by a bomb exploding in the hall,
by a dark spot on an X-ray.

Bless how the cardinal sings his morning call
despite the rumors of the sky's slow fall.

—*Peggy Brightman, Quechee*

Back to the Beginning, Again and Again

for my VMN cohort

Most of the downed leaves on the old lumber road were brown,
gold, fading shades of red. We moved along
alone, in groups, students tasked to observe, looking down and
    around,
tracking the low stone walls for gaps and patterns,
here a stretch of slender upstart birches, here a double-
    crowned spruce
planted a century ago by a house that was no more
a house.
       We were learning to read.
              Alphabet, words, easy
sentences—trees grow here in neat rows:
someone sowed them. Here is a ridge of hand-placed stones:
someone tilled nearby. The forest with a scar through its heart
showed its past to us, laid flat like pages, weathered furrows
just legible. Then, the teacher bent to pick up a twig. Fresh aspen,
green leaves still affixed. *There*, she said, pointing up—
up where we'd forgotten to look, a whole set of unread volumes,
open to P, for *porcupine*, round and black against the white sky,
eating its way along another road, over our heads.

—*Jennifer Brown, Montpelier*

Stepping from the Cemetery

Too full to write
I carry you with me
footfalls breaking crusts of snow
beneath a blue sky of sunlight

Birch curves echo
a white pine's shimmering reach

Insistent ravens
shout over the subtle calls
of chickadees? kinglets?
a small, warm, and darting thing

—Mark Brown, East Calais

I miss the stars (you're the stars)

I blanketed the stars in your tears. Fainting,
falling in an expanse of swirling colors.
Soaking into the cradle, stretching this so-called reality.
Pull the edge, yarn unravelling in rips of iridescence,
spilling slipping, tangles of light. Pinpricks of brilliance
taking the place of your heart. And why shouldn't it?
Who wouldn't want the shine of a million million tiny points of fire
radiating from your skin. We'd call down the brightest,
second star to the left, follow the northern cross into the forever
and let the rest of the endless black crumble at the touch of our
        fingertips.

—*Lynnea Brunner, Richmond*
previously published online in 2022

Haiku Musings 2023

simplify
all becomes dessert
all the time

self
a lifetime learning
to let it be

catching fire
we have to toss it
to ourselves

adrift
slowly gaining trust
in the sea

nothing
I seem to need
more and more

writing
I can't stop knowing
I'll see

holding on
impossible without
letting go

snow flakes
softest of all
caresses

—*Cheryl Burghdurf, Middlesex*

New Neighbors

Feeding chickadees and tits has ensured
that we have had many fat gray squirrels
every long winter for years.
However, those black squirrels, sleek,
shy, elegant, and so very graceful,
are extinct in Southern Vermont—
at least, they were until recently.

First there was one, by our feeders,
and then last year a greedy couple.
Now in the rough, gapped trunk
of the ancient maple dying in our ravine,
there is a new family, old and very young,
coal black and playing on the rocks.
They skylark 'round and 'round our full feeders.

What is the measure of happiness
for a squirrel? Good company?
I know how to measure mine.

—AA Burrows, Guilford

The Departure of Fireflies XII

We make our way to the back porch
The one that faces the end of the day

Our eyes begin to assemble the unmowed meadow

Watch as it widens and grows
Past the silhouette of cedars

To where the hermit thrush sits
In the saddle of a tree
I can never find

We wait each night
For the woods to constellate into bright "I love you"s
That pulse through the grass
And touch the edge between the open and the beyond

Until finally

When all are paired and peaceful
Their alacrity unnecessary

We rise and navigate
The lifetime between
Now and next year

—*Ana Burtnett, Worcester*

Fade into Me

For years I tried to shed you
Move on, move away
A hard line will separate your pain from my flesh
New art, new love, new life
Music will be my skin

But time is a pressure wave. A ripple, a resonance

And My voice has your gravel
My melody, your path
My song, our story
And her story
And his before that

Our music, even after you fade away

—Jolynda Burton, Montpelier

Song for a Bird

Once in a forest
The friend beside me
Whistled advances at an innocent bird
Who thought they were writing love letters
And eagerly composed his best poetry
Only to be left in silence
When my friend was through with his fun
How heartbroken I was for that bird, searching for his
    mirror song
I hope he is innocent of the deception
That so many of us find hidden in communion

—*Kay Bushman, Berlin*

Comfort Zone

My Buddy he's my hero
He's so smart, slick, erudite
Regular on the editorial page
Advocates so cool and confident (like he really knows)
Who could not believe him?

I'm so thankful and awed
for the way my Buddy protects our petro stock portfolios,
removes any guilt that I'm still driving
my 9 mpg '09 Hummer, and points out how
it gets great gas mileage when I tow it on long trips
behind my 6 mpg motorhome!

My Buddy is so amazing the way he argues (with a straight
    face)
that Vermont's too small to make any difference
or that we'll all starve or freeze to death (or both)
if we stop burning fossil fuels (not the other way around)
Takes all that burden of responsibility off my back! Phew!

Funny though how my (really smart) Buddy seems to have
    forgotten
(or maybe just conveniently ignores)
that all life on Earth, including us, derives from and depends
    upon
the soil, water, air and all the natural resources
these threatened and degraded elements provide, nurture
    and sustain

But personal change can be so gosh darn messy and . . .
    what a bother!

So thanks awesomely Buddy for helping preserve (even for
    just a little longer)
my comfortable, oblivious, irresponsible, self-centered,
    petro worshiping life . . .
    to the end

—*Barry Cahoon, Danville*

Letter from the Meadow

I have been mating with the inarticulate world,
pressing my forehead into the bosoms of trees
till they yield to my love, flooding me
down warm dark where no words are.
The fawn under moss and berries at dawn
I see and am, and the stags
I bargain for with my blood,
into whose swift prints in the clay
I press the flesh of my hands.
The burnished breasts of the robins,
the spiders casting adamant ropes
across the abyss, spinning from center,
the snake loosing his skin in the wheatgrass,
sleeping under the fallen door
with the mole curved into his side,
not eating the mole:
these move me with joy,
move me into the light-shaken silence
in which the trees sing.
The yearling doe's dark mouth kissed mine
in dream. I am here to fall still:
when I speak,
it will be with many tongues.

—Calliope, Montpelier

Sharing juice in the shade

We rest under a tree and trade words
as prompts for future poems.
You give me petrichor; I can taste and smell it,
metallic and dusty, with a hint of sweetness.
I give you codes for my secret desire.
What I wish I could say is, I hold a space
for you—not a placeholder, you're not
a backup plan, rather, a parallel love,
someone for whom I am always longing.

We are a puzzle, you and I, never clear
nor straight, twisted in knots old and new.
You speak to me about the weather—
the thin sliver of moon or how many
winter layers you're wearing—I ask
how you've been and you say, "like an alien,"
or "surviving"—you ask about my home life
and I shrug the question away.
There is a language humming between us,
shouting affection and rage. One day,
we'll share this conversation out loud.

—Frances Cannon, Burlington

A Brief History of Blackberries

with a nod to William Carlos Williams

David bought and ate some—
all of them—before I arrived.
They were delicious.

Four days later, I have some
of my own (four-fifty a quart
at the Farmer's Market) I
eat them, one by one,
juicing them on the roof
of my mouth. Before
they even have time
to stain the bag,
I eat them all.

—Michael J Carter, Brattleboro

Yellow Birch

Yellow Birch
Roots look like Spiders
Spreading Seeds
Far and wide
Yellow Birch
Pioneering new Forests
Teaching us the reasons why
Regeneration
Relationships lead to community
Co-creation
Building New Earth
For the Collective We

—Rae Carter, Plainfield

Fox Contemplates Rabbit as God

To seek the dark root.
To curl against the coming days
like a rabbit,
lucky and unafraid.

To seek belonging
between the trunk and thigh of the world.
To have no secrets in that hour of grace,
summer's bounty balanced lightly against the winter's storm.

To augur the return of summer
by wind and love and moon.
To press your velvet heart against their dreams
and welcome all with sturdy joy.

To call out from your burrowing sleep
to the buds beneath the snow.
To teach them joyfully of
our ends and our beginnings.

Only you, little rabbit,
could make that kind of love.
Only you, with your shining eyes watching,
tender ears listening.

In your keeping, life and death become the same benediction,
one no more, no less than the other.

—*Shanon Casey-King, Hartland*

Standard Time

C'mon, c'mon, c'mon,
honk the flyover geese,
necks stretched out
with purpose. They fly their loose
communal V.

A single, raucous caw
from a high-perched unseen crow.
An answer from a far field.
Then silence. Assurance of some sort,
enough to carry on.

Their lives are crisp,
unwasted. They know what to do,
and when. Time takes
their lead, dissolves. Consider this
my caw. I'll just do what I do.

—Dave Cavanagh, Burlington

I Wonder If . . .

I wonder if my Mother will be waiting for me
when I get to heaven?
Will she stand with open arms as I run to them,
no longer a dream of that warm embrace?
Will my fifteen-year-old memory of her blue eyes
be the same face that is looking at me now?
I wonder if she will recognize the person
I turned into, not the rebellious teen who fought with her,
but the young bride, the loving mother and the grandmother?
Will she be proud of my accomplishments,
the hard-earned college degree,
the career I chose to help others and make a difference?
I hope she smelled the lilacs I brought to her grave
where she now peacefully rests.
Did she hear the stories I told of her,
the Avon lotion smell, her laughter, and badminton skills,
her soft hugs, the summer tan, and all that feistiness
packed into one tiny woman's frame?
I wonder if my Mother will be waiting for me
when I get to heaven?
I certainly hope so . . .

—*Debra P. Chadwick, Burlington*

Gray, the Haze

Empty, the beach. Strange, the distance.
Perfect, the sky. Rough, the branches.
Stiff, the sail, the small cries of joy
receding. Odd, the comfort now
grown over the disturbing smallness
of my daily life. Gray, the haze—
the mountains, ridgelines draped
like moonlight moths. I've signed up
for the pinging—positivity rate, bacterial
bloom, heat wave, hail, smog of faraway
branches cracking in flames. Dare I
touch? Dare I greet? Dare I wade? Empty,
the day. Perfect, the sky. Strange, the heart.
Gray, the cloud. Rough, the breath.
Dreadful, the distance.

—Judith Chalmer, Burlington

An ode to Max

Your eyes shine in the dark, oh sweet and fluffy one
Reflecting the light to yourself and back.

Lonely, you rub up against the post
as you walk past, ready to pick up where you left off

The moon shines down, but we cannot see
as you can. The tall grass where the black birds live

The inches under the black bearded snow
that is the only thing   protecting the mice

And as the sun rises you sit on our laps
all the time, with fascinating coolness. You sap our

attention from day to day things
all
meaning
less

—Ari Chapin, East Montpelier

Wonderful Moments

Oh Max,
the way you climb
up on the picnic table
and lick the butter off our plates.

The way you look me in the eye,
with your intent hazel gaze.

The way you follow me to the garden,
not on my heels, but I know you're coming,
to hunt and prowl along the fenceline,
or laze in the straw path with the sun on your fur.

Oh Max,
the way you always met us at the door,
climbed in our laps around the fire's open flame,
never afraid to share your warmth and invite affection.

Your playful moments—chasing string or straw,
your patient and stubborn way around little humans,
sitting calmly, with your ears flat back,
staking your claim until the torture was over.

The way you, as a kitten, would nestle
up on my shoulder, under my chin,
and even as an elder cat, still attempted that.

Oh Max,
such a wonderful long moment
with you in our lives.

—Ela Chapin, East Montpelier

An homage to Mom and to Dad

Fingers hovering over the keyboard
I reverently wait
to listen to dictation as, one at a time,
bedridden, side by side,
my mother and father craft their poems.

Mom, lying on her back with her eyes half mast,
Gently sways her knees back and forth,
smiling ever so sweetly, as she relays
soft quips and quirky details.
A deep belly laugh emerges as she
visualizes an especially hilarious experience
and we both laugh out loud.

I type in awe and gratitude
bearing witness as her ingenuity with words
graces the page.

And dad sitting upright,
speaking with clarity and precision,
a twinkle in his eye and
a furrow on his forehead,
recalling moments on the tennis court
at 90 years old, with a hint of pride and
well deserved embellishment.

In those moments of togetherness and purpose
we rejoice in the sharing of each others' creations.

—*Sue Chickering, East Montpelier*

George

Our wood guy shows up to dump a cord,
starts to explain about how he'd found
a dump truck on resale, repossessed,
but the problem was once he got it
to the mechanic it turns out
its engine was no good.
Scrounged up a new engine for it,
brought it to the shop, guy says,
"Oh, I can't put this engine in, your truck's
got a cracked frame."
As we chatted, he was telling us
how he's supposedly retired from
his work up at the hospital
but they still need him *per diem*.
Last month he worked near half-time.
A surgeon, he had to transplant a new
something into somebody.
She had to get sent by fixed-wing air ambulance
to Boston for specialized treatment—
only seventy years old.
Hopes she makes it.

—*Alice Christian, Colchester*

Love

Love, oh love, you make me smile.
Love, oh love, please stay for a while.
You make my heart bloom like a big Dandelion in May.
You make me happy every day.
Love, oh love, you're so nice.
Love, oh love, but I don't love lice.
Love is something pure.
Like when my best friend, Jada, opens the door.
Love is lovely.

—Lexi Clarfeld, age 7, Colchester

Pulling Up Courage

She slides easily into whirlpools of emotional dust,
Each particle a different shade of
Happy, disgust, surprise, sadness, fear, anger, anticipation,
    or trust.
Still ground beneath her feet, covered richly with fire kisses,
Cloud formations in the sky remind her of her ex-lover.

Her teeth chatter as satellites fly above those clouds,
Though heat from the kisses brings warmth from below,
Her heart shivers in ice air of past memory echoes,
That satellites broadcast about lies she wants to forget.
Reaching down into the roots of stone below,

She pulls up courage, knowing she will exit the crate
Of contempt he left behind in so many corners of her body.
Chalk one up for ME she thinks:
I will hide no more,
I talk to the clouds,

And they shift shape,
My heart will stir,
As I heal, I step forth,
I sing to the wind,
I cast the dice of true savory flavor
With no scent of sweet nonsense.
I am as free as the blue sky
Now.

—Peter Clark, Woodbury

Touching the dog

Some part of me must touch the dog
as I sit or lay on the floor.
Some part of me must feel the dog
that has burrowed under
the blanket or rug.
It does not matter to her—so long as
it is dark and warm underneath
and my back
is against her bottom
or my leg
alongside her head
or the soles of my feet
against her soft brown fur.
It only matters that our heat flows
from one to the other—then we are
content and can sleep or read
or scribble poems and
dream dog dreams
rich with yelping chases
and smells of rotting things.

—*Micki Colbeck, Strafford*

Cursive

World's Tallest Filing Cabinet, Bren Alvarez, 2002, Burlington, Vermont

We build our monuments in fear
that we will never be remembered.

This one in an old parking lot towers
like stanzas of an ode, our memorial

to fully articulated fingers, opposite
the thumb, which in concert, consign

our X. The Palmer Method taught us
rote ovals and sawgrass, right-formed

letters ending up ours. I'm amazed at
clear smooth streams of styled words

grandparents left me as family history:
script flourishes of T's and F's and S's

illuminating a person behind the pen,
ink letters like blood infused with life.

I am speaking in straight Palatino 12,
my signature scrawls, anxiously ad lib.

—Philip Coleman, South Burlington

but what of ten eyck

At last, a woman on paper.
—Alfred Stieglitz on Georgia O'Keeffe

but what of ten eyck
the lighthouses, Ida, they are
metaphor, angles of light,
casting the same shadows your sister lived under. she,
whose kaleidoscopic talent eclipsed your own,
wandered through a dry-gulched desert alone,
while you traveled a teeming sea.

of her, he said, "At last, a woman on paper."
his was the lusty idolatry of the muse,
no compliment, her burden.
while you, dear nurse, understood the artistry of healing,
heard the language of light, these endless
symphonies of refraction were your safe harbor.
ahhh . . . yes, lighthouses,
standing sentinel above exposed rock,
you, their painterly sister,
recognized in these singular soldiers,
a quiet, steadfast worthiness,
more alert to the changing of the weather,
to the fickleness of men's hearts,

the steady beacon you would become,
the quiet chronicler, painter, nurse, and lighthouse keeper,
each piece of you with so much more to say,
with the pull of every tide, the waxing and waning of the moon.

—Mary L. Collins, Lake Elmore

After Covid

When this is over, what will you do?
My mind flashes to
the velvet green of baseball fields,
rare burgers, hot, crisp fries,
the long trip home—my life, my friends.

But then I ask, "Is 'over' even possible?"
For years the pain of earlier times returned
in waves tsunami-fresh:
my mother's cruelty,
the heartbreak of lost loves,
marriage to someone married to his work.

Now that I am old I realize
that "over's" not the lethe of forgetfulness,
that pain and aftershocks of pain endure,
but unlike death itself can lose their sting,
turn simply into
lessons learned from memory.

—Ann Cooper, Middlebury

Song Astride

I dared again to sing this morning,
loud and wide—And without warning,
rushed pleasure's uninvited twin—
Struck from without and from within.

I remember how it was before,
one natural note was call for more,
full out for miles and miles on end,
fair moments, and naught to amend.

In puddles during Summer Showers,
likewise we would splash for hours—
When Gift of Fate aroused, we'd move
in shared and solitary groove.

~

We long, because our breaths are numbered,
to lift our spirits unencumbered,
and sing, in unobstructed voice,
our songs by chance, if not by choice.

~

A feat of Grace to sing astride
the reaches of this damned divide,
a trial of the shattered heart
to string together what's apart—

And carry, within a single chord
more Joy than our Sorrow will afford,
the melody rising all along
to lend itself in return to Song.

—*Linda Corelia, Montpelier*

Ghazal #11: The forms that "Alone" can take

We'll speak, whether we are together or *alone,*
of the many ways that there are to be *alone.*

Down the windswept fenceline the crossrails are missing
and now the remaining post has begun t*o lean.*

Days since the injury . . . How it adds to her pain
she must be the one to rub on her ow*n aloe.*

Bold! Steadfast! Our solitary pillar of strength!
Tell us, who can this be other tha*n a Leo*!

You know, you shouldn't find it strange that suddenly
no one seems to know you when you come for th*e loan.*

Sitting here, long after my buddies have gone home
to their wives, now the barman's eyes tell me: *No ale.*

High in this oak at autumn's end, most leaves have been
gone for a week. How sweet to be that fin*al one.*

Having wrapped me within this snow-softened stillness,
the empty street now brings the gift of *a Noel.*

It can be hard to recall I'm not on my own
when I hear that saddest of all songs "Nich*ael, no!*"

—*Nichael Cramer, Guilford*
previously published in *The Ghazal Page,* #76

Awe

It's a shiver that climbs the trellis
of the spine, each tingle a bright white
morning glory breaking into blossom
beneath the skin. It can happen anywhere,
anytime, even finding this sleeve of ice
worn by a branch all morning, now fallen
on a bed of snow. You can choose to pause,
pick it up, hold the cold thing in your hand
or not. Few tell us that wonder and awe
are decisions we make daily, hourly,
minute by minute in the tiny offices
of the heart—tilting the head to look up
at every tree turned into a chandelier
by light striking ice in just the right way.

—James Crews, Shaftsbury

Load Shedding

Hey child
Do not assume connectivity.
Hey child, Unplug sometimes.
Please learn basic math,
Punctuation, and grammar
Though it may bore
Thee speeding mind.
Study atlases and learn East from West.
Please value sunsets
And learn how to bake biscuits.
And did you know,
At night when the lights
Go out, it is easier to follow
A path barefoot?
And to be quiet
Beneath the stars and between the fireflies?
Hey child, Millennial,
And whatever comes beyond
Fresh to the Earth
Turn towards it.
Turn towards the soil
And all the bumblebees
And butterflies.
Download the Moon.

—*Jezebel Crow, Woodbury*

"The Master's Conceit—Spring Evening"

Who would sorrow alone in the springtime?
Faced with this you must drink straightaway.

—Li Bai, tr. E. Eide

Li Bai, you look so weary. All the wine
is gone. It's just as well—another cup
wouldn't extend the night a minute longer.
Somehow you staggered down these ragged stones
with no one to lean upon—another miracle—
to let your feet dangle bleeding in the stream.
A bowl of gold coins glitters on the water.
Ignore them, poet. Lie back instead and gaze
at the high moon on his watch. How much more wine
has he had than you? Composing lines
in your head about the joys of drink and women
although you're alone and weeping, certain that
the moon's verses are putting yours to shame
as he sings to the faint stars gathered near him.
And not a word will you remember, come the dawn.

—Ralph Culver, South Burlington
previously published in *The Seventh Quarry*, Summer/Autumn 2022

Hometown

Olvidada pureza, como quisiera rescatar
ese dolor de Buenos Aires. Esa espera sin
pausas ni esperanza.
—"After Such Pleasures," Julio Cortaza

Never the same—your loss, its lack
—the hometown, childhood city,
neighborhood, barrio, doesn't understand
itself without you. The abandoned buildings
of your youth have lost track of demolition,
bullied into making way, in a lost year,
for strangers—the new, the better:
Randolph Elementary, American Legion,
even the church—you, an altar boy,
first house—childhood home you remember,
gone.

Only the oldest buildings stay, gone some
to repurposing, but your barber shop, drug store,
pizza place, all lost to history. You remember
Merusi's, on the corner of Merchants Row and Main
—always dark and cool, girlie magazines in the back,
penny candy, only soda fountain in town—coke syrup
and carbonated water, soda water long before
you knew carbonation—five-cent cup.
That was your town, and it's gone.
You could have stayed.
You couldn't have saved it
anymore than it could have saved you.

—Douglas K Currier, Winooski

Alphonso

I catch him in the corner of my eye as I pull into Shaw's in
    Montpelier.
A big man stands at the exit, he has an American flag draped
    over his backpack, he's holding a cardboard sign, cars roll
    by, looks like slim pickings.

It's cold out now.
I hurry in to buy a few things, by the time I'm back out and
    in my car it's too dark to read his sign as I pull up to him.
    He's carefully rolling up his flag. Rolling the window
    down I hand him some money, I used to think this was
    encouraging bad behavior but what evidence do I have to
    back up this theory ?

Thanking me, he mumbles something about the flag and
    politics, he's missing a few teeth and hard to understand.
I ask him his name, Alphonso, he says it clearly.
I tell him mine. I reach out to offer a hand, he starts to fist bump,
then he grabs my hand for a shake, his hand is
rough and worn.

He says, "I'm not a little boy, I am a man."
Goodnight Alphonso.

I turn right to home; what would I miss
if I keep the doors locked and the window up.

—Whit Dall, Montpelier

The Star of David

The Star of David is way out of sight
It used to be sparkling, shiny and bright
Somehow it has been hidden by a dark hovering cloud
As if to be ashamed and wearing a shroud
I cannot seem to see it no matter how hard I try
I keep pondering over and over as to the reason why
I know I must have faith that it is all part of God's plan
But it is so very difficult for me to understand
I can sense and feel David's overwhelming pain
And it is extremely difficult for me to refrain
From nudging this star to stop hiding in fright
But rather come back to us and make the dark light

—Corinne Davis, Montpelier

Pearl

Look, the result
of a natural defense
against an intruder,
whatever will damage,
hurt the small soul,
the soft-bodied creature,
oyster or mussel inside.
The mollusk captures,
coats, covers the trouble
layer upon layer
with iridescent nacre
made from aragonite,
calcite, binding conchiolin,
Hold it up to the light,
see light itself
broken down within
shining depths — reflection,
refraction, diffraction.
You can tell the quality
by the hard, lucid surface,
the refined luster of survival.

—Greg Delanty, Burlington
previously published in the *Atlantic*, April 2022

Take, Eat

I stuck my finger in the burning hot
Air pocket of an under proofed ciabatta
The sensation was instant
my finger enflamed
Being some place it didn't belong
This immense empty space
The kind of space only yeast could create
In walls only gluten could create
Structure
Flour water salt yeast
Surrounding my finger.
I think about all the times I have
Been hurt by this bread
Been burnt by this bread
Become a part of this bread
This bread a part of me
Bread
My body
Take, eat

—nd dentico, *East Montpelier*

Greif

I have trouble spelling grief.
It's an awkward, rarely written word
with a backwards set of vowels, I think.
I've only recently had need to use it quite a lot

The I
never seems to want to go first
to be in the center, standing alone
between "GGGGRRRR" and "What the EF!"

My I doesn't want to become
the breaking point
that no-way-back decision
that axis which becomes reversal

A fault line, an unraveling center
around which spins a child's top
and the innocent remembrance
of everything ever forgotten or lost

Rather the I in my greif
seems to want to stay with the F at the end
As if there could be another outcome, a different choice,
a future tense

My greif seems to always want that other possibility
to be preserved within it.
IF
Is more like the way my grief wants to be written.

—*Ren Dillon, Berlin*

Shape

Magazine clipping: twin girls,
joined all but neck, head,
could run, coordinate arms, legs,
no one knows how.

The coordinate points of the heart
are determined by shared light,
no one knows why.

Geese design an arrow in flight
somehow know
the shape of the whole.

The arms of Oneness enfold you
if you could get but distance
and close enough to know it.

—Arlene Iris Distler, Brattleboro

Triolet to Spring

New sprung movement, measure so sweet
Woven language banish my grief
Away from melancholy's deceit
New-sprung movement, measure so sweet
Office sacred, chorus complete
Sacred moment, a fresh motif
New sprung movement, measure so sweet
Woven language banish my grief

—Mariessa Dobrick, Barre

work from home

the dolls gaze at my back
as sun sets outside my window
their arms raised to the sky
in surprise
the marionettes place wooden fingers to their mouths
in silence
the possum hasn't spoken all day

—Small Doris, South Royalton

Skeletons of Iron and Stone

I have seen a rusted, half buried plow
Behind which a life was spent
With back bent and sweat on the brow

I have seen a quarry filled with water
Iron loops that once guided pulley lines
Now smoothed rings holding the roots of trees

I have seen the remnants of a military fortress
Its stones scattered and scarred by gunfire
Today touched by the soft hands of children

Among these skeletons of iron and stone
Our ancestors labored, lifted, and resisted
Farmers, granite workers, soldiers, journaliers

I like to imagine they once paused to glimpse a day
When their child's child's child
Would walk amidst their old confines

Finding memories and appreciation
Of lives that came before
And new resolve in the rubble and the rust

—*Jared Duval, Montpelier*

Things I Forgot To Tell You About

Fire Flies
Strewn across
The back field.
Surprising
And
Unexpected
Bursts
Of
Light.

—Kathryn Eberly, Montpelier

Inside Waves

it's the kind of sky
that muffles time
and steals the day away

white foam fingers
comb cottage clapboards
for storm-tossed treasures

inside, I hesitate
coffee drained, shoes ready
steps away from the sea

but your door—still closed
sleep pressed
against the hinges

I untie laces
settle in my seat
no ocean enough

without you

—Ann D Fisher, Lincoln

Mistral

Hold onto the napkins, plates, table—
we'll eat this food that cannot be blown away.

Outside the sun is so hot it tightens the skin
around my mouth. It's a *mistral*

the diners say between bites. In my neck of the woods
we'd eat inside in such a gale.

Here, at a friend's home in *Le Barroux*,
we dine *à l'extérieur* to savor the shaved *truffe* in the *omelet*,

the local wine. So, open your mouth.
But the wind reaches in first with its fist,

and steals your breath. It's the kind of place
that reaches into a longing you didn't even know

was so close to escaping your lips. Longing
for what? To begin again, here? Rosemary

and lavender growing wild
along the dusty roads, mollusk shells

underfoot, far from the sea
to be of this place.

—Nadell Fishman, Montpelier

An Encounter

A rustle in the leaves—that doe again.
We look up at the same moment, attentive
and still. She stares. I stare. She's not ten

steps away. I murmur, *It's okay, I
won't harm you.* She flickers her ears, and when
I whisper again, she comes closer. Why

does this keep happening? Maybe she knows
something, thinks I might know it, too. I try
to tell myself I understand. Her nose

twitches, testing my scent. I try to tell
myself the truth about these woods, unfrozen
in time, ever transforming. The elms

are gone, and the catamounts, but the pines
and the oaks and the deer are doing well
for now. I tell myself that she's a sign—

of hope? of trust? or what? The woods are dense
with unending change, eternal fine-
tuning, rebirth—not things, only events.

—Michael Fleming, Brattleboro

The Something

Time to notice drops of dew
on every fallen leaf,
to draw a finger through the tiny pools of light,

to watch a body's shadow
casting backward on the leaves,
to feel the sun's surprising heat,

this late October day.
Time to feel the veil of—something—
the *something* that exists

between me and her, invisibly pulling,
as I sit in sunlight waiting
for a single leaf to drop

so I can catch it mid-flight.
I can feel her texting—*please bring mushrooms,*
I want to make a soup for you.

—Laura Foley, South Pomfret
previously published in *Alaska Quarterly*, Spring/Summer 2022

Winter Window

Iron-cold icicle columns cling to the eaves and hang long
like the thick bars of a jail cell over this two-story window
if I choose—

pain is part of life but suffering is optional   like how blood
is the most spectacular shade of crimson.

If I talk to myself like   a beloved friend
place my hand gently on my breast   feel the downbeat
of my own song in my own chest   and tell this little
      instrument
how much she is loved   I might actually start to
      believe it.

So when I look out the window I will choose to see
how the sun plays on the icicles like a   crystal concerto
how the   branches of the birches sway in the breath from
      the hill
I will remember that this impossible arrangement
of molecules called me
uses small spheres in my skull as optical devices
to translate scattered light waves
of   every possible color
into these   translucent chandeliers
into this   ballroom of white snow
        bright as hope
and I will believe I am not an accident.

—*Debra Fotheringham, Waterville*

Morning Walk

Just out to the garden to take the sun full face,
to feel those long ago mornings of owning first light for
    myself.

I remember the day I first answered a cardinal's call.
Pete had taught me the trick of tongue needed
to whistle back again and again. I stood still,
my red sneakers dew-wet in tall grass,
my Grammie sweater snugly buttoned.

I recall once being alone with only a squirrel
running round and round the telephone pole
for all his own reasons, until a shiny brown beetle
crash landed on a blue cornflower right beside him.

Many mornings the maple leaves hung patient
in their thousand thousands from those Great Green Beings
in no need of motion like mine, as I twirled my plaid skirt
so fast it flattened out around me, The Spinning Queen.

Remembering is the work of the old. We awake and begin.
Sometimes we weave in gaudy threads of invention,
but usually, like Penelope, we unpick those
with a sigh that same night, making,
remaking, not knowing just when
we'll be done.

—Sarah Franklin, Montpelier

The Greatest Gift of All

Could it be the sun
that rises each morning

as if it had spent
the night kneeling

behind the mountain, or
is it the squirrel

that gleefully lurches
from feeder to feeder

as if the seeds
were put out for him, or

in March is it found
underneath the snow,

a crocus waiting,
bound to a promise,

the greatest gift of all.

—deb franzoni, Castleton

Tenders

shadow puppets of children
eating peaches and pomegranate
(it's not their season)

our shadows
grace flat december walls
(our season will come)

up these walls
in crimson purple echos

when i am shattered by grief into slivers of myself
the red and jeweled shell of my beloved is water bearing,
     tough, and filled with sweetness

time spreads, weaving heartbeats
in the in between of a winter's breath

then, ashes lay lighter than the snow
and seeds wake up to their desire for light

—Graham Frechette, Northfield

Physical forms of love

Sandra and Winnie
Physical forms of love
Two women from Ghana
They are here for us
Night and day
Brushing mom's hair slowly and carefully
Looking into her eyes
The daughter she never had
The love she always wanted
When she got older
And felt lonely
Staying up with me in the kitchen really late
Listening to me
Being my real friend
Cooking the traditional fufu so I can try it
When I tell them to take the 25th of December off
So they can celebrate
They say "no—
This is how we celebrate!"
Sandra and Winnie
Physical forms of love
Two women from Ghana
Teaching me how to love

—*david fried, Montpelier*

Cleaning Out the Car

I smudged it with fresh sage from the garden.
I was afraid to go back at night.
Afraid you'd come out.

Looking for the cigarette lighter, I found:
your teeth
two pop-in false teeth, on a little metal retainer

Your plain brown pony-tail holder, used masks,
 chapstick (don't want to catch your scaly skin).
A bag of half-eaten chips, a half-drunk water bottle.
A datebook, tissues, toothpicks, quarters for meters,
 canvas bags in your colors, deep forest and army
you might crawl out at night

Wondering at the gas station, what kind of gas? Read the manual.
Your *favorite* thing was to drive around, all day.
So you would want . . . your car to be on the road. This sacred car
you would've never let me touch; I touch it now, while my mother
cleans out your apartment.
I faced it all, the over-crowded trunk, the grease.
but the teeth only come out at night
you can't donate that.

I couldn't believe I was strong enough to drive your car,
to put it out of mind like where meat comes from.
There was no other option: you were not here
to drive me

—*Gaia Fried, Montpelier*

Zeh Ha Yom

"When you were born you cried
And the world rejoiced
Live your life so that when you die
The world cries and you rejoice"
—*Cherokee Proverb*

The day before *Bubbie*, my mom's mother died, I got on a plane.

I brought my guitar and sang her favorite Yiddish song.
She clapped her hands and sang a few words with me

I kept waiting to see her eyes—chocolate brown pearls of
    wisdom—but they remained shut.

My father said, "You want to protect your kids from hard
    things, but you can't always do that."

I like to think I can take death for walks on a short leash—
put it in a box and store it in the attic—filed separately from
    my LIFE folder.

I like to think my weather app will save me from tsunamis—
and chocolate will protect me from grief

If Bubbie saw me cry she would say, "Shtay oof! Stop moping
    around!"

Her favorite psalm reads "Zeh hayom asah Adonay nagilah
    v'nismicha vo"
This is the day G-d has made, let us rejoice and be glad in it—
like how the mourner's prayer in the Jewish tradition praises
    G-d.

Even through the great depression, even through the holocaust,
even through my grandfather's death, she thanked G-d for
      each day.

So too must I see the sparks of light she gave me
and hear her say, "When the going gets tough, the tough get
      going!"

In honor of Shulamit Weisman 4/16/1928–01/03/2023

—Navah Liora Weisman Fried, Burlington

Long forgot

Sitting in the fading light of day,
storm approaches not far away.

Silence fills the darkened room
waiting for the thunder's boom.

Like a burden laid upon our time,
quiet solitude not so divine.

So blessed although we cannot see
what's before us this gift so free.

Reflect upon important things
some day gone that's what life brings.

Be thankful for what we've got
some day gone and long forgot.

—Marcy Frink, Worcester

The song we sing

Is there a sound? Is there a song?
Is there a move? That moves your soul.
A song that uproots you, that makes you fly, that makes you
    ground yourself to the max?
Is there a song? Is there a love that makes you scream, scream
    with joy?
Scream with rage, scream with song, scream it all from your
    whole core.
They will remember.
They'll freeze the bully.
They'll have to walk straight to hell.
They'll disappear into the unknown, while you stand tall.
They won't be back because you planted.
You planted love and strength and it sprouted
It sprouted here and everywhere.
It sprouted love and transformation that makes you hopeful
    and dope.
There is a movement that is healing now.
A song, a move, a storm of hope
It makes you fly
It makes you whole
It makes your story
True to the core
The song we sing is of resistance and of the fire in your heart.

Porque hay canciones que no se cantan
Solo se viven en carne propia
No se repiten, no se repiten
Solo se viven

—*Amanda Lucía Garcés, Montpelier*

Drip drop rain falls down

Drip drop rain falls down,
Drip drop rain falls from my eyes
Full of joy.

—Edda Gitnick, Grade 2
  Rumney Elementary School

The tiny burden of her death

after a poem by AD Hope

                  r i s e
I expect birds to   in the air
effortlessly,

                 untethered
by gravity or grief.

Was it a miscalculation of velocity,
or a moment of distraction
that caused a flurry
of black feathers to tumble
across the road,

      s c a t t e r
then   in the sultry air,
quiet as a prayer?

—*Andrea Gould, Plainfield*

Damage

If you saw what I saw and just what I saw,

You might have thought there were little specks of something

Floating in the patio light's beam

And if you had an 11-year-old's inquisitive nature,

You might have walked from the rec room toward this strange
    phenomenon,

Awakened from your transfixed state

Only when there was a shattering of glass inches from your face,

And the shock wave from your knee reminding

There was a sliding glass door between here and there.

—Dave Gram, Montpelier

Blackwood

Late afternoon,
any Summer,
kneeling in the backyard,
poking the ground to make
a bed for yellow and orange
marigolds, I hear a sound seep through
open kitchen windows, sonorous
underwater bubbles, rippling wrinkles
on a laundered sheet, quickening to a ringing
call to God or to a lover, luring even
the bee to stir from the tiger lily blossoms.

In the growing shade of the Rose of Sharon, I listen,
charmed for so many hours, years, by ascending
and cascading melodies made by my husband's
breath that brings to life mpingo, the hard black tree
of Africa. Caught from air, just air, songs
and songs arise. From bone of wood a wind
alive blows through the house from one
end to the other, swirling out
back windows, out front doors
where even the children
have stopped running
and are quiet.

—*N.G. Haiduck, Burlington*

When

When her friends
started dying
they followed each other
so closely
As though they had beckoned
one another

as though all her friends
had climbed
aboard the same train
beginning some wonderful journey
leaving her behind

She hopes when the time comes
when her world grows dim
and silent
she will hear the train's rhythm slowing

the whistle blowing

there at the end in the red caboose
her friends will be gathered
hands outstretched
urging her to clamber aboard

they will pull her up to join them
in a different kind of house
that rolls over the land

with nothing beneath

—Wendy Hale, Montpelier

Morning, Kaneohe

grass meets jungle
two lanais below
the lofty porch, dark leaves
glistening in early light.

goats mutter on the hill;
ecstatic bird chorus
floods the woods;
music fills all spaces,
replacing thoughts.

the hand and moving inky brush
trace vines, avocado trees,
papaya, the spiked gold and blue
Bird of Paradise.

breezes blow banana fronds
together and apart, sibilant, raspy,
trailing fringe, whispering and nudging,
gentle as lovers.

in a small tank an axolotl paddles tiny feet;
her body moves with sinuous grace.

Now ! light floods the facing cliffs,
volcanic fingers
splayed to hold the day.

—Amy Handy, Montpelier

The Inherited Creed

I am burdened with the creed, the need
to be perfect in all I do. It is the in-grained

belief passed on from Mother
who expressed aloud her trust as other

women before her had, for her family to be perfect.
She tried with her mighty will in every inch of her perfect

body to cause that to be. As her daughter
the firstborn, I did my best to oblige Mother.

Last Sunday from a woman my age I heard she,
too, got that message—I heard this at her perfect tea.

No boy child gets that dictum. Instead, he
is applauded when he breaks the mold, speaks

up, rebels a little, is comic in school—
he's taught it's manly to be cool.

—*Kathleen McKinley Harris, Charlotte*

Unconditional

for Dayton

In a barrage of blistered beauty,
between psyche and psychosis,
through bent and battered glimpses,
where barren dreams become
seed scattered;
like monotony and monogamy,
we are multiplied but first divided.

Heart beholden, I call you friend,
one of my eternal tribe.
Settled into, seized in the knowing,
that we, tenaciously tethered, are
sipping on the soul of more and none and still
together, stumbling,
flipping time the finger.

I am a splinter of you,
here, cradling our creative chaos,
the destruction of all that is and isn't.

—Tracy Haught, Montpelier

Surface

at the door
wolf waiting
moon in Leo
my daughter
looking for
the lost cat
beneath the
maroon carpet
the cat is missing
and the world
swept off its feet

—Mary Esther Hayden, Marshfield

There is enough poetry in the world

There is enough poetry in the world
There is enough longing, contradiction and juxtaposition
Plentiful, gaining on exorbitant juxtaposition

There is metaphor galore
Ample make the bed—for
Somewhere, somewhere there is a fat cat sat
On a mat

There are granite stones marked with a hand, one finger
        pointing to heaven
"We hope to meet again"
There are sufficient reminders of our short journey here

There are enough seeds of doubt, beauty and rage
For every being to fill a page
There is enough poetry in the world
And not enough poets

—Elizabeth Heeter, Williamstown

To Survival

Each night—
children asleep,
dishes done and dripping dry—
you chill the wine,
and we make a toast.
"Survival cheers," you say,
and our glasses clink.
What it means
just to make it through a day
has changed,
its value way up
like the price of oil
or gold,
rising like
a hot-air balloon
buoyed
by nothing more
than fitful flames
and luck.

—Jen Heller, Montpelier

Nibbling a lemon scone

Nibbling a lemon scone,
you wonder, are you older now, or just old?
Your oldness strolls
with no hurry in her feet
through milkweed meadows and goldenrod,
having left the garden to the bees
and the sun's dappled nod.

The early moon comes up curved
like a crack in time
and you blow your breath through yellow flowers,
calculating the years
between probable death
and the surprising eagerness of "now."

And you release your calculation like a pet snake
into the rocks and flowers at your laces.
Having wandered to the hidden places,
having succumbed by the hour to autumn's revel,
you lie down in the unveiled scent of earth,
where your oldness takes a nap in the cardinal cradle.

—*Kathleen Herrington, Montpelier*

Felt Like Writing

felt like writing
so I went to my favorite bench in the park
where I often go to write
but by the time I got there
didn't feel like writing
so I didn't write
no one was watching anyway
but things change
& I felt like writing
so I started to write
when this park attendant
in a uniform with glinting badge
on her cap turned & barked at me:
"No writing in this park!"

—*Geof Hewitt, Calais*

Everything I Know About White

Caucasian white, the calico cat's white,
the white of the notebook page, broken
by thin blue lines. Veined white quartz
gravestones. The ivory bill
of a woodpecker once thought extinct.
The white of black-and-white: TV
before there was color. White of a poached egg,
white of an eye compromised
by hard living. Bright white of a New England
clapboard house, so bright it looks
like color. The candle's white flame,
the hot white center of fire, the white light
of lightning and the white heat of anger
splayed against a neon bar sign.
The white place your eyes go to when
there's nothing you can have
so you go inside yourself, harbor it there.
The white pages of the books that saved you,
the powdered faces of the teachers
who saved you, white chalk dust clinging
to schoolyard brick. Chalk dust drifting
down the blackboard, Mrs. Costello
writing the true things in her perfect letters,
showing you a script as bright as the Milky Way.

—*Nancy Hewitt, East Randolph*

Nocturnal Neighbors

If you enjoy a stroll beneath the moon
near places where the woods and water meet,
you're likely to encounter a raccoon
that's rummaging around for things to eat.
With bandit masks and beady eyes they creep,
but really there's no need to be alarmed,
for even though they might disturb your sleep,
these furry rogues won't do you any harm.
They're happy eating fruits and nuts and frogs,
serene by rippled water, quiet plash,
but also crave our scraps and food for dogs,
and go like hellions tearing through your trash.
With nimble fingers skilled at any task,
they'd probably play piano if you asked.

—*Sam Hewitt, Essex Junction*

Society creates the crime

Sometimes on the ground, I'd find a twenty,
blowing in the wind. I'd call that lucky.
But no one carries cash no more. So where
did all that luck go? A wing and a prayer—

when everything is all AI, they hack
without a gun ("stick-em-up") in your back.
Society creates the crime, they say.
That's one way to see it. But if I may,

I'll add another view: It's not just crime
they go about creating all the time.
Hallmark, for one example, made up "love."
I must admit that when push comes to shove

I wish they'd never done; they make me feel
as if this broken heart is really real.

—*Cindy Hill, Middlesex*

Cedars of Summer

Old Cedar trees line the shore where I swim
Tall dense and lacey they reach skyward
Tiny Cedar cones cluster together in abundance
Touching the water with their essence
As the Summer solstice nears I swim everyday
Breathing in the swaying cedars
Breathing out songs of summer
I sense the cedars' lime green undersides
 As I swim underwater below their reflections
Some mornings the wind and rain stir their stillness
 I am invigorated by their natural movement
After months of swimming with my cedar buddies
The cedars show rusty brown needles of autumn
I hold this gift of oneness from the cedars of summer
As the cedar needles fall and snows of winter hail

—Alicia Hingston, Danville

Because It's Spring

Because it's Spring
I can now exhale
the darkness that has
clung to me like frozen rime
ice around the edges of my skin
I can open my arms wide
and lean my face
into the warm reassurance
of new life

—*lily hinrichsen, Bristol*

Metaphor Tree

There's an old Sugar Maple on my morning walk,
marking the downturn in the road, covered

with bumps every six inches . . . cancerous carbuncles,
reminiscent of leper colonies, though they're called burls:

abnormal tree growths caused by extreme stress,
like refugees sacrificing everything for freedom,

lined faces testifying to hard labor in fields,
disease and poverty—so many lives lived in pain,

and yet, this spring, the tree leafs out
like all the rest, green flags hiding

the bark-covered boils,
a prayer, secreted in the human heart.

—Sarah Hooker, Marshfield

Postcard from a Stack Tied Up with Twine

for my father R. B. E. (1929–2001)

I've got a stack of blank postcards
and I'll be writing to you soon.
I picked them up in town. Both sides
are blank. There's room for words on one
and room for art on the other—
all just waiting to be filled in
so I can send them off to where
you are. How long, now, has it been?
I'll save some change on stamps. It all
adds up. The weight of losing you,
the decades now, the things I'd call
to say to you but can't and so
I write. We said, I remember,
we'd stay in touch. Wish you were here.

—*Mary Elder Jacobsen, North Calais*

The stream

You knew I was ready to jump
 so you pulled away in time
Too big of a commitment for a boy who is scared of his own tides
Your actions hit you hard but not with my lottery stones
I never want another flow
You already took mine
Now you have another stream
And I know I should be jealous of her
But I can see that smile of yours and
I know it's for the best
You've taught me how to be
 See the beauty in simple things
Starting from gestures to the color of the streams
I am becoming a better me
With every piece of art I see
 So when another flood will come
I will be ready with my heart

—*Karina Jagodzińska, Montpelier*

Well Being

Let us be known
for the plea, sea to sea—one country,
lakes, plains, city streets,
essential work rewarded
long past pandemic disease.

Let us be known
for questioning, inventing,
justice boring through
smokescreens, through hate
berating those dragging their bones
as the richest gain riches.

Let us be known
for opposing those
who sharpen their claws
on a daughters' plea
for a new economy
steeped in well being.

Let us be known
for clearing the sky for better lives,
now and then—an extra slice of pie,
known for the falcons' wingbeat
freeing seas of hungry children
as the raptor's shadow passes
dropping bills like uneaten seeds.

—*Judith Janoo, East Burke*

Clifford & the Cassowaries

on June 26, 1956, world-acclaimed trumpet player
Clifford Brown was killed in a car crash.

an old tenor man sat me down   one brilliant
autumn day   & told me a story of a saintly
wildman.   a real tragedy,   golden
brown,   was a poet   & a sculptor.
how he   worked brilliance into   brass,
how he captured   the sun
in a mouthpiece.   O' how he   blew!

the ritual we call   rhythm, the twist
of it,   the pull.   his palms could press
honey from wax,   & horn that preached
of coming day.   when he spoke
the roaches sung, & land would hum, & snare top
shake.   O' how he   blew!

but bird flew   how high the moon,
& parker pranced   with giant leaps,
Clifford would be lying   embraced in
tarmac.   wings clipped   at twenty five,
trumpet echo   in the void.   so he walks
with the cassowaries now,   to forever yearn
for open sky,   so his monolith stands
as he does not.   O' how he   blew!

—Emmett Jarvis, Montpelier

Remembrance of Things Past
(Mangoes not Madeleines)

I pop the lid open on the glass jar
and the pungent smell of bagoong hits my nostrils,
carries me away into memory

For Proust, it was petite madeleines
that brought on the sudden recollection of things past:
A cookie dipped into a warm cup of tea
His aunt's home in Combray
The town square where they went for lunch

I scoop the dark-colored shrimp paste onto a plate,
peel the green skin off the mango,
slice the pale yellow flesh into inch-wide segments

I am taken back to Nanay's dining room table
covered in thick plastic and plates of pork barbecue
I hear the voices of my titas and titos
telling stories in the language of their childhoods

I am transported by the taste of hot tropical sun
and briny ocean foam

Suddenly, memories and ancestors are alive on my tongue

Maybe Proust was right:
Smells and tastes are like souls
ready to remind us of what we once forgot.

—*Joan Javier-Duval, Montpelier*

Vernal Contrast:
White Wisteria and Flowering Locust

Beautiful white racemes
dangle delicately down
from a hidden backyard
wisteria arbor while,
on a parallel street,
poor man's wisteria appears.

In plain view, for all to see,
other white racemes
dangle delicately down
from furrowed gray-brown
barked black locust trees.

From the same Pea Family
the blossoms of both
the woody vine and tree
are fragrant and frequented
by the indiscriminate bee.

—Wilma Ann Johnson, Bennington

B for Brave and Bold

B	I	N	G	O
B for brave and bold. A woman who went blind from too much seeing.	**I:** Integrity. Independence. *Never* allowing another woman to clean *her* house.	**N** for negotiations: Always one to offer a distraction from pain, ill-ease, or too much fun.	**G:** A Grand Matron of Lodge and Love.	**O:** Her smudged mouth —her win or not.
10		37	46	Small porcelain balls rattled in their metal cage while she sat perched on a folding chair jawing sticks of sweet-stinky Juicy Fruit chewing gum and raking her blunt fingernails across a worn tabletop. And always, the white-p o w d e r e d donuts sat at the ready—me, licking my skinny-girl lips, waiting for my number to be called.
The way I remember it, Great-Gramma Annie started the obsession: Two thick red ink blotters carried in her brick of a pocketbook. She wore the sueded-leather bag like a weapon under her crepe-paper arm.	22	★	I took to the BINGO fever at a young age. Gramma Annie and I played in every basement of every church in every town.	
	19	43		
20	39	55	64	

—*Patty Joslyn, Montpelier*

Mid-June Morning

I followed a silk line
running for miles
fingers wanting to graze the trail.
Little slugs raised their antenna to watch
blades of grass bend under my feet
until I found the matrix of a spider home
covered in diamond dewdrops,
flag waving within fog
rising from the riverbank.

I wanted to know—
   Are slugs snails without homes?
   Did the spider release the silk to find its foundation
   or leave a trail to find its way back?
     Am I the spider or the slug?

—Robyn Joy, Montpelier

Agog

The first time riding a Schwinn I was flying
air scraping cheeks flooding ears
slabs of sidewalk edged with crabgrass rushed beneath me
ankles flapping like new wings
knees quick, supple as grasshopper's

fenders clattering building speed
spinning to the end of my small-town block
trailing a wake simple and keen

then   buried in tree shadow
heaved sidewalk seen too late
the earth pulls I resist strain suddenly feral
haul on the handlebars
stomp on the pedals

swerve like a kite
into braided winds
aloft agog intent
launched

a lifetime
riding bikes
Fleetwing Salsa Firefly   airborne

—Karen Kane, East Montpelier

Being Your Mom

My arms were made to be open,
ready to give hugs and hold you tight.
My body was made to nurture you,
to nurse you, sometimes all day and night.
My heart was made to love you,
to be everything you need me to be.
My soul was made to be your mom,
to discover a whole new part of me.
Being your mom is who I am,
and while I am other things too,
there is nothing better in this world than being a mom to
    you.

—Natalie Karlin, Colchester

Morning Plum Blossoms

I breathe in morning plum tree blossoms sweet
and white. I close my eyes to morning dawn
Dewy plum blossoms aroma complete

The fragrance so happy and full—replete
with love like a frolicking playful fawn
she prances about little and discrete

Under the flower moon of spring, we greet
the pregnant potent lilac bobs a nod
Dewy plum blossoms aroma complete

and watch colors arrive wonderful treat
the morning wakes up artists colors crown
the days delight my heart a single beat

the dappled woods wink morning shadows meet
Daffodils blossom beaded morning dew upon
every spring blade of grass a new green beat

a young birds nest the baby's distinct tweet
blindly seeking nourishing light so spun
I breathe in morning plum tree blossoms sweet
Dewy plum blossoms aroma complete

—*Monda Robinson Kelley, Brandon*

Nothing fancy

Just the Montpelier bike path
not a walk along the Danube or the Arno.

But the pile of dirty crusty snow
the "Beware: Poison Ivy" sign, soothes me.

Cracked black asphalt, salt stained
loose gravel unearthed by the plow

ski tracks in leftover snow on the fields
that will soon host soccer, ultimate Frisbee

ice chunks floating in the Winooski
taking their time to Waterbury and beyond.

I am masked, sunglassed, scarfed,
sun barely able to find skin, but I feel it.

The law of here and now
right now, is to just be.

And wonder: *What is the smell of spring?*

—*Renee Kievit-Kylar, East Montpelier*

World Voice Day, April 16, in Ukraine

The goal of this day is to raise awareness of voice problems and help people who have them

Can you hear the baby cry through this dark night?
  No, this baby died in a cold basement crib.

What of the grandmother who watches her husband,
    nephew, and son buried in rubble?
  She cannot speak.

The militia soldier covers his face with a green mask.
  He fears to say his name.

Video shows a neighborhood fallen apart, destroyed.
  What voice lifts this?

The radio broadcasts a spokesman's announcement from
    the other side.
  What did he not say? Do you swallow or choke on lies?

A youth chorus assembles in the intact city square.
  Listen for missiles and patriotic songs evaporate into rain.

A couple married fifty years stare at night's constellations.
  Stargazing does not require comment.

Do you hear wind in branches of the oldest oak?
  If you are lucky. If the oak remains.

—Tricia Knoll, Williston

Everything Pantoum

Everything is linked to this
day you were born
which split my life
into a before and after.

The day you were born
was elation, was exhaustion
splitting life into a before and after.
Before, I slept whole nights.

Elation and exhaustion
existed as expectation.
Before, when I slept whole nights,
I dreamed of you, a baby who

existed as expectation,
which split my life.
I dreamed of you, a baby to whom
everything is linked.

—Samantha Kolber, Montpelier

It is an Act of Love

written at the start of the COVID-19 pandemic

It is an act of love,
I would think,
as we switched off our high beams,
coming nearer each other,
the roads darker in Vermont
than anywhere I had lived before.

But this, is the ultimate act
of love, our receding
into the closed doors
of our homes, not seeing
each other, keeping away from
those we long to be near.

It is an act of love, we say
out our windows, into the night
(Venus, you are there) hoping
the others will somehow
hear, hoping to just not be
forsaken now. We are here,

right here, just hidden—subtler
humans, less bidden. It is
an act of love, and love
more ubiquitous than we
imagined. We will remake
the world—with care.

—*Carlene Kucharczyk, Woodstock*

Haikus

(1)
Certain stars do wait,
    take with them the night, the dark,
shine when it's time to.

(2)
Steal the stars again,
    constellation's pickpocket.
Any good dreams thief?

(3)
The broken moon hides
    nights bodies from lunatics,
love from massacre.

(4)
Whistle sweet tree ghost,
    your pains and cuts in the dark,
tune each bark's crevice

(5)
Whispering violence
    humble is the carnival,
under snapped tightrope.

—Christopher Lawless, Jeffersonville

Disappearances

Rapt, an old man inspects his living room mirror
but not for his image. Instead, its angle
subtly reflects the light of a stub of candle
on the silent piano. He might say the reflection shimmers
but the years, though blessed, have jaded him some.

He'd rather avoid such a hackneyed word
but he's also abandoned the urge to think up a better.
A train comes to mind, though he doesn't know why.
He can't recall when it was he saw it or even
if, but it seems some caboose's lantern

lodged in his mind a lifetime ago, its glow
growing distant. Was it even then a matter
of things he longed for fading? The rattle and click
on the tracks make a poignant song. He'd rather
ignore its meaning, clearer now than ever.

—*Sydney Lea, Newbury*

Contemplation

The silence is the deeper
For the music
Bach, Beethoven, Handel
Pouring forth
Cadenzas
Codas
Heaven
In an earthly shell

—Maxine Leary, Montpelier

Flying

I was flying through the sky one day
looking down at the beautiful bay.
I look up into the starry sky
wondering how it would be to fly.
Then I shoot up through the dark
Like a tiny little spark.
And in the corner of my eye
I can see a bird that flies.
Then I fall down into a dive
Shooting across the sky.
Over the sea and hills I rise
Over the stars I migrate South
And shed a little tear.
Off I fly shedding all my fear
My time North is finally done for the year.
So I wave goodbye to all my friends as I fly away.
And then dawn breaks the dark to shreds.
A new day has begun
And I am here.

—*Emilyn Leinen, age 9, Colchester*

Arguable

for Goldstein

Who wins our competition?
You accuse me of excessive sensitivity; I call you a bully.
You say I am irresponsible but I think you need to play more.
Might you be a know-it-all or am I inexperienced in need of
    education?
Maybe I have my head in the clouds;
It could be that you don't dare to dream.
I blow sunshine;
You rain on my parade.
Right side up, upside down,
Forward rolls, backflips,
Dizzying cartwheels in both directions,
Reversible hurled insults our gymnastics routine.

—carol k leinwohl, Colchester

Power Out

Power out
All day and night
Cozy with candles
Spilling their light

Winds howl
Rattling window frames
Woodstove glows
With warming flames

Staying home
No trip to town
Phones strangely quiet
Internet down

Faucets sit idle
Pump can't run
Snow melts in buckets
Dishes get done

Neighbors trudge over
Despite winter's might
Sharing Shabbat-akah
A night of lights

With morning comes thanks
For our roof and warm bed
Power's back on
Enough's been said

—Michael Levine, Middlesex

Streets

The streets of my city
roll over rivers, past buildings
trees and tennis courts

The streets of my city
have seen hearts by the hundreds
poems to ponder
bicycles and buggies
feet, hooves and wheels
bodies of hunger and hope

The streets of my city
have heard music and murmuring
sirens and screaming
goodbyes and hellos
rain rush and thunder roar
whispers and sleepy silence

The streets of my city
have tasted chalk and paint
tar, oil and blood
cigarettes and sorbet
snow, fog, and pollen

The streets of my city
have drowned in floods and grief
and marched in sunny celebration
and just keep rolling along

—*Cynthia Liepmann, Middlesex*

veil

with humor and fantasy
trickster and demon

serpents and all manner of beast

with storm, flood, fire

with metaphor and mundane
with adult, kin, stranger and child

dreams

unwrap unconscious wounds of trauma

expose blind spots
and illuminate to comprehension

reveal portals to unknown possibility

excavate self
from false perception and expectation

dispel abandonment and loneliness

awake unconscious
to knowing

mend survival into understanding

carve loss into grace
vulnerability trust compassion

what deception
next to be unsmoked?
what veil to be lifted?
what deeper self to welcome?

—Hugo Liepmann, Middlesex

Oh Lord, Spring Soon

Oh Lord, spring soon
Sweep across this mean white landscape
It presses upon the warp and woof of our lives
 and forges our desperation
We are marrow cold and bone weary Lord
Condemned to huddle together cheek by jowl by lip
Muttering feebly against winter's vigorous contradance

Oh Lord, we know spring is gathered
Poised and virginal
Please spoon the earth
And seed the restless, sentient land
with your milk and honey kisses

Lay your miracle makings hands on

our boxed about bodies so pulpy and sun starved
our blush blue toes and fingers
our cold pressed psyches
our echo chamber houses, smeared just yesterday it seems
    with the sun's warm fingertips
our wait for tender shoots of kissed air breezing against
    our faces
our need for a boozy ramble through fertile fields of born
    again green
our swollen memory of too, too many days cast in snow
our neighborhood streams crying for warmer waters
our felt hope for the early arrival of emerald colored trees

—Bob Lincoln, North Middlesex

newtonian physics

all is quiet this sunday morning
but for the millions of crickets,
which have been going non-stop for weeks now.
while sipping coffee,
reading poetry, on the back porch
an apple hits the rusty-brown tin roof
of the old house and thumps to the ground.
still standing, though listing badly, it's in rough shape.
the foundation of the once grander house sits nearby;
they say it burned to the ground on another sunday—
the parlor stove set the place ablaze after church.
the tree has grown since I built my house here 24 years ago;
it was too small for its branches to sweep over the roof
when a family of seven lived there in the 1920s and '30s.
two rooms, one upstairs and one down.
life must have been filled with the
the smells of mama cooking sunday dinner,
the sounds of we kids playing,
of papa playing his harmonica on saturday night
as we sat on the stairs and sang along,
keeping time with a wooden spoon on a pot,
eating popcorn,
all of which would have drowned out
the sound of a green apple hitting our roof.

—craig line, Calais

Morning, After a Great Snow

The flaws of careless daily management
Lie hidden under soft, forgiving white,
An ermine cloak aesthetically arranged
Over an aging, mottled, spectral frame.

We never seem to get this landscape right.
The driveway's ruts and humps, the weeds and stones,
The branches shed when wind assaults the trees
(which someone should have picked up at the time),

The gardens full of weedy stalks and stems,
Beds cluttered with old vines left there to rot,
Instead of tidied, raked, and neatly mulched;
Until the spring, no one can see our crimes.

I let the dog out in the quiet air.
The shadows of the trees make streaks of blue.
The wind has blown the fresh snow into shapes
That curve like fishes' backs or mermaid tails,

And covered all the flaws and failures up,
A respite from the ceaseless push and prod
Of till and plant and weed and mow and tend,
Of rake and prune and paint, repair and mend.

There is no hurry in this crystal globe;
For a brief pause, until the plow trucks come,
Only the beauty of this still, white space
Sculpted with no help from my hands or will.

—*Gina Logan, Braintree*

Cold War

19 soldiers
ponchos flapping in wind,
perhaps they're at Chosin Reservoir
perhaps on Heartbreak Ridge
       winter war   Korea so cold
they slog on through ice and snow
each clutching his weapon
Frank Gaylord's sculptures
neither alive nor dead
frozen in time
like war that never ended
magpies fly over the border
quiet now in the DMZ
where they nest in maples
so many dead there
some left behind
a mere dimming
between life and death
as sunlight fades and night grows cold
   war
19 soldiers frozen in time

—*George Longenecker, Middlesex*
previously published in *Sixfold*, Spring 2023

What Steps to Take

My steps are not the bear's, lumbering through forest ferns,
pressing their weight, clawing bark, reaching berries,

nor are they thin prints of fox, arrow to the wind, swiftly scouting
land for mice and moving food.

I am not like wolf, masking my hunt around stands of trees
and brush, waiting for prey.

Who am I, daring to travel in this moss covered land, that my
kind have separated from, without asking questions.

I know nothing.

How do I walk so as not to disturb, listen so that I do not disrupt,
sit quietly so that all creatures

and plants around me, are free to fly and run, sense
that my presence is not a threat.

That I will not squash partridge berry under my feet,
take a birch to the ground, leave burning coals from
a warming fire.

And like any home that I enter, not dismantle the
woodland altars that have spirited the caves and
spaces with their grace.

—Jesse LoVasco, *East Montpelier*
previously published in *Windblown 1*, 2022

What You Came to Deliver

So, you
        fumble
for words
            straining to find
the right one   the word
you came to deliver

not seeing how
          the stumbling is
its own beauty.
You can not know
where the search
is leading   or who
you are becoming as

the word
begins to draw you   to itself
as it puts on flesh
and stands with you
in solitude
where   your only choice
is to speak
the inexpressible,
making audible
the frequency of your heart.

—Ray Lowe, Worcester

Seed Catalogues

I gather seed pod dreams and promise
From the mailbox: each day a new crop,
Colors popping live from the page—
It's catalogue season, sure enough,
Drop kicking post-holiday blahs out
With the new year . . .
Johnny's to the rescue! Gurney's!
White Flower Farm, Gardener's Supply,

Every page redolent of spring sung dreams,
Of flowered perfection, of smiling
Women in neat trousers kneeling,
Nary a spot of dirt upon their knees.
Page upon page promises: long warm days,
Happy people glowing with abundance.

They've no shame, these
Dream purveyors, hustling for
A hopeful gardener's heart—even
Charming tots, chubby faced, glowing,
Grow pumpkins big enough for a carriage!

Why not succumb to bouquets
Of perfect sunflowers clutched in tiny
Hands, beckoning from the page?

Ah, catalogue dreams,
Seeding hearts with spring.

—Veda Lyon, Worcester

My Colorbox View

A pure blue sky
Above the steep hillside,
Where trees have changed
From green to gold.
Lower, below this color,
Is Route Two
With its commerce
Of semis and service vans,
Bright traveling billboards.
I watch this parade
As it stops and goes,
In sync with the
Red Yellow Green of
Traffic lights that
Organize this flow
Over Taylor Street Bridge,
Its Green geometrics
Spanning the Winooski River,
Water, Nature's Mirror
Reflecting All I See from this,
My One Window on the World.

—Sandra Maccarrone, Montpelier

The Way to East Corinth

The churning water found its way
Between the icy rocks to play
Hide and seek among the trees
Beyond the gravel road.

The buntings and the jays were perched
On the limbs of maple, pine and birch
Piping sunlight down the ridge
To gild the valley floor.

Woodsmoke from the farmhouse stove
Hid the field and tightly wove
A blanket for the village green
To wake it from its sleep.

There stood I awhile yet,
And in the waning of the Winter met
A whisper in the thawing land
Of the music of the year.

—Michael Madill, West Topsham
previously published online in 2019

The Ruins

Watching over you
in room 4060
on curve 25.
Let's get some air.
Primal cries set against
a backdrop of
sea lavender and purple roses.
Standing by your side in
midnight gardens
at the grave.
I got to hold you
in your pain.
Baby keep your head up.
I'm reaching for your hand,
until the end.

—Kimberly Madura, Essex

Another Beautiful Day

Occasionally I find you there, alongside me again
riding in the seat next to mine
a ghost with a scarf covering your hair
on a beautiful day, beneath the blonde bob an actress
from a movie I am watching wears,
in the high staccato laugh
or toss-away phrase I hear
from the woman seated a table away.
All the years that now demarcate us
immediately bridged
long enough to re-present the wound—
until that, too, fades away
as the separate voices of Canada geese
blend into a single note
drifting south in the middle of the night.

—Tony Magistrale, Burlington

The Dead Were Still Dancing

It was a financial decision,
they said, to quit the mowing
at the hillside graveyard.

And the grass hardly had a chance
to stretch before the town
began to cry and shout:

"Who among us still cares
for our lost? And how long
will it be until the weeds
bury them once more?"

The deliberation ensued
long into the summer
nights while I'd sit atop that hill
and swear

that the dead were still dancing.
Just above the tall grass
like starlight. Fireflies rising

and flickering among graves
that they'd always known
as their home.

—Jack Markoski, Montpelier

Charted by the Stars

To the stars, do we look like stars
as we buzz around in cars after dark,
stopping only for traffic lights?

I want stars to see me when I am
by a bonfire, sparks sending signals
coded by my celestial body that say:
My bones are made from your dust.
My compass steers by your trusted revolutions.

What if I could grow so bright
that I rewired electricity
to the frequency of sun drying a leaf,
so brilliant that the internet's algorithm
remembered itself as a prayer
from the ancestors?

—Lisa Masé, East Montpelier

Nesting Dolls

Mother Robin nests every spring
under our carport and raises her young.
There is singular purity in her love,
devotion driven by need,
by evolutionary obligation.
She knows more about her robin world
than I could ever understand.
There is no dissuading her.
She loves like her mother,
and her mother, back to a mystic beginning,
like a series of Russian nesting dolls.

Our love, too, is a series of nesting dolls,
my love nested in yours,
my hopes and dreams nested in yours,
our brief shining moment nested in time.
One generation in another, in another,
enduring companions we carry genealogy
with the constancy of the Pole Star,
the devotion of Mother Robin.

Some say nesting dolls invest us with good fortune,
others say they are the grandmothers.
It matters little what grace we grant these carved and
        painted figurines,
for all the grace they grant us, for all who come before
        and after.

—*Jack Mayer, Middlebury*

I'm not in love with growing old,
my once athletic body round with living,
sore with the scars of exploits past;
My mind scattered, mixing the old and the new,
into dreams of forgotten places, times, people.

Hopes and dreams for the future are replaced
by a growing appreciation for the here and now.
The perspective shifts from the distance
to the foreground, and that's fine.

My life today is enough—enough food,
enough fun, enough music, enough friends, enough.
Adventure is replaced by concession,
with acceptance.

I'm not in love with growing old,
but it's enough.

—*Charles Mayhood, Calais*

Rush Hour

Short-lived, this beauty sweeps
across October sky, treetops on fire,
a flash of crimson bright outstretched
in redwing blackbird's flight.

Who is all this blazing for?
Were I not gazing up just now,
who would catch this sight,
that slight tilt of scarlet feathers
colliding with autumn flame?

Still, even in the bleakest landscape
light spills across empty skies.

Still my chin swerves upwards,
drawn by wind and trembling leaf,
alert to feathered summons:
Look.

Now the bird drops from sight,
sunlight wanes, chill of evening stirs.

From far above
snow geese veer south,
their cries filtering through traffic

like prayers for every being
facing downward
dimly rushing home.

—*Katherine H. Maynard, South Burlington*

Self-Storage

It's not really the self that's in there—
more like all the forgotten parts of your life
you intended to revisit:

the swimming trophy you crawled miles to win
or the gold stars on a third grade calendar
marking the few days
of the one week in your life you behaved.

Then there's those pants
you think you'll sweat yourself back into.

They lie folded among the paste trinkets of time,
the jewels of your memory.

But what if you could . . .
just cinch up the whole girth of your life,
then flatten your beliefs
right out of your gut

(ironing out those wrinkles you keep stumbling over)

and fold your whole kit and caboodle of a body
(brain included with all its loose connections)

into some old snakeskin suitcase lying around
with its rusty lock and faulty hinges, then wait

the long humble moment it takes
to, at last, be carried away?

—*Tim Mayo, Brattleboro*
from *Thesaurus of Separation*, 2016

Lost Dog

for Finn

I'm wading through the shock and grief
of finding our dog dead on the floor.

He left us in the night as if he'd
run off, on the track of some wild

creature drawing him deep
into the woods beyond our call.

Lost forever, yet I still call
for him to come home to us

and retrieve the joy he'd left
behind now in shreds, scattered

like all the toys he ever owned.

—Elizabeth McCarthy, Walden

Looking for Work

No need to make things up,
only the need for work, a job,
something to pay the rent,
Rustling through the papers each day,
barely hoping.
And this is what I find:

Female exotic dancers.

Manager wanted: moving to new, happening space.
    Only the responsible & enthusiastic need apply.

Marijuana and tobacco smokers needed for university
    research study. (Smokers of both.
Comp. Up to $775.)

Dancers $450 weekly paycheck, tips & commission.
    $2-3k weekly.

Adoption

Casting—TV series seeks people struggling with painful
    addictions, esp. danger,
video games, steroids, promiscuity, plastic surgery.
    Also seeking troubled teens, desperate housewives
    and groupies.

Get paid to Shop! Mystery shoppers need to pose as
    customers.

Adult entertainment producer looking for new female
talent for future productions.

Bronze casting, welding, construction. Buddhist Center
seeks full-time volunteers to help build large temple.

—*Florence McCloud, South Burlington*

Birdwatching with Dad

Dad is paused attentively in the quiet kitchen
His green eyes following a pair of wrens outside the window.
Purposeful, officious, enviably single-minded
They dart in and out of the birdhouse hand-painted all those
    years ago
Finding just the right twigs, flying them back, puzzling them
    through the opening to make a home for their young.
He's probably washing a dish, or drying one off, or slowly
    pouring hot water through his coffee grounds
The window is open a little, hinting at summer life that
    chafes the edges of this quarantine
The backdrop the wide green lawn of the backyard
he has mowed a thousand times.

382 miles away
I hesitate at my back door with Sam on my hip
Watching a young male cardinal hopping over our bricks in
    the bright sunshine.
He jumps awkwardly, unafraid, gamely alighting on the
    clutter that fills the space—the baseball tee, the hanging
    pots, the plastic kiddie pool.
A flick of his tail stirs the afternoon heaviness, a chirp
    breaks the silence that comes every day but that still feels
    uncharted.
I've started looking forward to seeing him
He's a child soother, a jester, an undaunted optimist, a friend
    in this time of distance, isolation, mourning
A connection.

Dad and I
Finding the movement in the stillness
Watching the birds.

—*Megan McConville, Montpelier*

21st Century Blues

Lonesome cuz I got no friends
Hungry cuz I got no teeth
Wasn't always this way though
But life goes screaming by—
And no one wants to help you move
And no one wants to hear you cry

Metal parts replace the real
Older, no wiser, or even mature
Not easier, harder, most of the time
With cutting, pasting, staples and stitches
Now all of the seasons are full of wind;
Ghosts, banshees and wicked nice witches

Prayers or curses for Heaven or Hell
But whatever it is that you hold dear
May be gone when you turn away
Cuz now All Souls is every day
As too many of the dead and dying
Wander through every reality, crying

—*Maggie McGill, Montpelier*

Sleight of Hand

Save the gossip among chickadees
and blue jays, the sweet empty promises
of a few brave robins more confident than we are,
and a cantankerous crow who wants in on the secret,
the woods are silent as mud boots by the back door,
expectant and impatient for the burble of peepers—

liquid green chorus resurrected
from the decay of years past,
undisciplined joyous song
that seems to go nowhere
    and everywhere
all at once.

Winter will finally yield, ceding flotsam
and jetsam left in the wake of its tides
to the magician that is Spring—
white rabbit jostling her satin hat
as she pulls bright scarves from sleeves
before eyes ready to believe anything.

—Becky McMeekin, Braintree
from *Bones of Gratitude,* 2022

Precarious

My friend said last night that
she's hoping her life will soon be over;
it's been a while
since I've been that unhappy.

But I haven't forgotten.

For a long time now
I have not woken up
already heavy with dread,
which makes it easier
to throw back the covers and
expose myself to the day.
It might be
my attempts at meditation,
but I don't really know—
better not to analyze,
afraid to break the spell.

No, I haven't forgotten.

—*Joanne Mellin, Winooski*

The Good Olive Oil

I want the good olive oil.
It's hard to help it when the dark
Bottles crown my cupboard so proudly,
When I think about the metal jug half my size
That had its own cupboard next to the sink,
That I'd squeeze between my thighs to pop
The spout, that smelled like rich, golden summer,
That my mother painted in crosses atop our door frames,
That I rubbed into my hands like lotion and soaked
Up with bread like ichor.
Like rich, golden summer. The way the leaves splashed
Shadows across the small table and the breeze
Smelled of birdsong and soft dirt and a world warmer
Than the one under the supermarket fluorescents.
I want the good olive oil.
The one in the glass bottle that smells
Golden like my mother's hands.
The fluorescents shiver.
The plastic bottles are three dollars cheaper.

—Dahria Messina, Greensboro

snowflake shadows

when I lived in the woods
it seemed that every winter
I would learn something new
about snow and ice. the different
flakes of snow, the crusting,
the slushing, frozen footprints
in the path, ice crystals in
snow holes. the stream
and how it iced over,
how the snow covered that
with dips and holes where water
continued, the ice and snow
its blanket, the icicles forming
wine glass bottoms where
they touched the water.

many things and variations
on those things, and tonight
in my second winter in town
I noticed that the falling snow
in the streetlamp light casts tiny
shadows on the blanketed street.

as I looked closely at the smooth whiteness
I saw them, falling before the fall
waiting for the flake that was theirs.

—Bob Messing, Montpelier

Who Cooks for You?

"Who cooks for you? Who cooks for you?"
the barred owl asks, perched in the pine.
But, really, she prefers to dine
on fresh-killed game, perhaps a shrew . . .

. . . or, better yet, a juicy rat,
a squirrel, a mouse, a tender bat.

The wild barred owl has untamed taste;
her favored meat is never boiled
nor baked, nor fricasseed, nor broiled.
A gourmet chef would go to waste.

"Who cooks for you? Who cooks for you?"
the barred owl calls, but all in jest.
She hoots, and whoooo's; she puffs her breast.
Then: swoops, to strike, and seize and chew.

Who-hoooo-who-hoooo!
Who-hoooo-who-hoooo!

—*Christy Mihaly, Calais*
previously published in *Light*, Winter/Spring 2020

Searching for a lament

Yo-Yo Ma the great Cellist
played a lament for those who are suffered so much in
    Turkey and Syria
he has no blankets to share
jackhammers or bulldozers
he repeated many melodic phrases over and over
eyes closed a musician accustomed to going deep inside
was struggling to find his way
to go somewhere
the bow of compassion on the strings of reality
as I sit here having coffee this morning before coming to
    meet you
and read some of my poems
I wonder as I have on other occasions
the balm of art
the place of love traveling such distances
the everyday missed opportunities to help others
as I struggle to reach out today

—*Steve Minkin, Brattleboro*

Catedral

Catedral de Justo, Mejorada del Campo, Madrid
Don Justo Gallego Martínez

If prayer were an assemblage of bricks
These are the hands that would render it real

These are the shoulders that would bear
The brute tonnage of faith

Just as bones obey the will of muscle
Some part of him can't help but articulate

The heft of God

His soul agitated by a knot he can't untie
He frames out the armature of his belief

Into a chapel made of rust and refuse
Replacing air and absence with steeples

And altars roughly troweled in concrete
His ragged shirt dowsed in a libation of sweat

Blood printing its rich stigmata into every stone
Of this prayer made manifest

These are the walls and windows of one man's
Furious supplication left incomplete

The roof of his basilica unfinished, open to sky
So that birds wander through unburdened

And even the rain sends its congregation inside

—*Phil Montenegro, Montpelier*

In Celebration

The farm dog appears on the hill
barks, snarls, teeth bared.
He rushes forward, darts in,
snaps at Gillie. I scream at him

Gillie barks at him. He snaps
bites at Gillie's tail. Andrea steps
forward. "Don't get between them,"
I yell, afraid the dog will bite.
She's not deterred by him
coming at us, mean as winter.

By sheer force of character
she leads him back up the hill.
to the farmer then plucks long
strands of Gillie's tail from the
road mud, lays those wisps
on the snowbank, a shrine
to our fright, to her success.

Gillie and I are here to tell you
there are heroes in our midst.
We never know when
we are lucky enough
to walk alongside one.

—Nicola Morris, Plainfield

Dutch Interior

Frame your life
in miniature:
have a window
open to illuminate
just one corner—
a shoe, a stool,
a bowl on a table—
and show the cracks,
the mottled wall,
the way the cloth
falls in sunlit folds.
And all the rest dark,
darkness and shadows
where something may
move or not, or be
nothing at all.
Cup your hands:
held enclosed
all life is art.

—B. Morrison, Brattleboro
previously published as "At the Museum" in *End of 83*, Fall 2014

This Day

The frost it bit the morning glories
It took out all the squash
The flowers of both are wilted now
Their colors soon awash

But I will gaze upon them still
I'll witness their demise
For where they go I soon will follow
Yes, all that lives then dies

We die together or alone
We die in bliss or grief
We die, we die, we don't go on
Our time on earth is brief

But I am here right now, right now
And I will bless this day
With all my heart and all my might
'Tis here, right now, I'll play

—Lava Mueller, Randolph Center

Between Worcester and Elmore

Every fall I look forward to seeing
    the changing leaves along route 12, between
Worcester and Elmore, because it is
    the best place I know of for
Celebrating the wonders of the season,
    so as the leaves begin to change color
I take my first round trip to check on
    how things are looking in
The early stages of leaf transformation,
    then visit again after a while and
See the beginning of tree transformations
    when many of the
Leaves have turned colors, giving hints
    of what the peak of color will be yet still
Managing to keep it a secret,
    and then I return again on a sunny day
To find myself surrounded by intense shades
    of yellows, oranges, and reds
Everywhere I look, as trees that are adorned
    in bright leafy coverings merge
Into a flowing presentation of breathtaking color,
    as far as my eyes can see

—*Joan Murray, Worcester*

Before Work

It's not complicated
It's a relief, in fact,
To not face new decisions
From 6 to 8 a.m., instead:
Boil water, make coffee,
Add cream, compost grounds,
Brew herbal tea in a thermos,
Do dishes, make bed,
Eat breakfast,
FaceTime dad,
Pack bag,
Walk or drive to work.

If I'm lucky, I meet you first,
Speckled gray hair, sparkling eyes,
Gentle conversation,
Queer joy infusing the day,
Gratitude, my prayer and
The vehicle of my wellbeing.

—Poa Mutino, Montpelier

Haiku, baby . . .

Chapter ten in which
the sun scatters its suns on
the floor of the woods.

Haiku II, baby . . .

Chapter twelve in which
the runes of the birch reveal
all they know to you.

—Chris Nevin, Moretown

The Wall

I'm right up against it
And have been for weeks now

When I try to turn away
My cheek gets pulled to it, like a magnet.

I'm all boxed in, no way of escape.
Can't blow it up, or chisel it down

Shatter it piece by piece
Can't ever even leave it alone.

It needs me too, it doesn't work without me
We might be partners in crime

All I can do is seek redemption or refuge
Fall to my knees, surrender to the humiliation of
    attachment

Change the story:

So I push my entire back against it, knees at right angles
Hoping to train my body to accept the pain, the burn of it

After a few weary decades, I lean against it, smoking
as James Dean might have,

I can rest, finally, in support even
It isn't going anywhere.

Father, I can still feel your hand at the small of my back
Guiding my first wary bike ride.

If I grow back to that size again
Perhaps then I could simply step
over it.

—*Kevin O'Keefe, Brattleboro*

Silent Snows

I can't do it
I can't forget
The feeling of nighttime
In the city
When everyone is just starting to go out
In the city
With makeup so thick
It hides every hint of ugliness
Until the mascara runs down your cheeks
Under the hot lights
Dancing to "Vogue"
With some people you know
And some people you don't

But under the same moon
With no makeup to hide the ugliness
In Vermont
You can still ski across the field
In Vermont
In January or February
During vacation
With nobody else in sight
And the sounds of the owls
And your skis
And the silence of the snows

—*Carla Neary Occaso, East Montpelier*

Bilingual Tankas

雨に濡れ決めかねている鱒百合よ花でいようか魚になろうか
soaked in rain
trout lilies
can't decide
remain a plant
or become a fish?

芝刈りの代わりに蜂の羽音して No Mow May の街花盛り
bees buzzing
uncut grass
No Mow May
my town
in full bloom

夕暮れの光の中で輝けるコロナを共に生きし人々
on the stage
of twilight
each one of us
lived together
in a Covid world

籠をさげ八百屋のごとき森に行く今夜は行者大蒜スープ
as if going to market
with a basket
it's the forest
for dinner tonight
wild leek soup

—*Michiko Oishi, Montpelier*
(English translations with Judy Chalmer and Rhea Constantino)

It's Tough Saying Goodbye

The sand harbors hapless hulls
rushed and washed by gentle surf;
We lean against two boulders
tall and rough and lasting;
Near hemlocks embrace,
oblivious to our lamentation.

Remember that first day
sitting in the campus garden;
You were reading Hemingway,
For Whom The Bell Tolls you held up.
Fitting I think for this divide,
this moment of concession.

We parse the past, Time ordained;
The sun narrows its grasp,
spanning parallel rays
revealing a fault in the stone,
drifting east to west
giving in to its own falling.

A warbler sings a sweet song;
I stand up, still as the receding light,
stumble up stone-by-stone steps
stalling at the top,
turn and walk away—
It's tough saying goodbye.

—*Richard Fischer Olson, Montpelier*

Grandmother's Fire

This is our Grandmother's fire
    mingling prayers of sweetgrass,
        cedar, tobacco, and sage.

Made from a hot ember
    dropped by your keen whirling hands
        into a dry bird's nest.

Quicken the flame into your heart,
    feed it your holy breath,
        your laughter, your tears.

This fire calls for peace,
    For healing the planet,
        For speaking truth.

The spirits are listening,
    the fire's sacred words
        are the spirits' food.

—*Eleanor Kokar Ott, Maple Corner*
from *Heart-Work Trilogy: Words Out of Time*, 2020

You're Enough, Child

Hiding under a rock
Dirty in the soil of my sin
Wrapped in a hug of my insecurities
Worrying about what could have been.

Searching for something not there
Empty, drained and soulless with despair
Until I found you.

Jesus, you saw my light
Reached out a hand and gave me sight.
Dug me out of my grave
And gave me a home to stay.

I only know half of my heart
but you drew the full shape.
I'm living the chapter
But you're turning the page.

Jesus, you are all I need.
My soul is satisfied with your love
You feed my spirit with morning's bread
You quench the drought in my head
"You're enough, child."

—*Hannah P., South Burlington*

Never Alone

Trapped and lost, it all seems too much to bear
The walls closing in all around me, as I struggle for air.
Not sure who I am, or who I am supposed to be
A happy life seems so distant, inevitably far away.

Encased in darkness is where I find myself often
Doors closed all around me, my life story shut.
Voices in my head that just won't stop criticizing
Spinning round and round in despair, I've almost given up.

I fumble around to find some light, searching for my way
And realize it's my own voice screaming out that I'm doing okay.
Searching for some truth, a purpose, as I sit in the dark
So desperate and alone that I begin to pray.

I know of a God but He seems so far away
Reserved only for good people, and that's not me today.
How could He care, and love someone like me
Battered, stained and full of scars—how could that be?

But on my knees, face down and with tears clouding my eyes
Choking back anger and fear but feeling so desperate inside.
Longing for a freedom, something much bigger that I can't see
To just simply take the wheel, and drive forward for me.

I cry into the night, *"God, please take it all away!*
My deep pain, my past, all of the darkness inside me!"
As I open my eyes, a peace washes over me I've never known
And a gentle whisper from God saying, *"You're never alone."*

—Valerie P., South Burlington

Fish & Farm

You won't teach us to farm
like you cabbagehead Englishmen
when we've got knotty nets
like neon stockings
mended too many times to know
what color they were at the start.

We push off the coast
to the turquoise field
and plant our hooks
seeded with juicy bait.

Here where the fish only bite for us
the men come home when the clouds
squeeze the sun across the sky
like pink icing on the cakes
behind the glass of your pastry shops
on the cobblestone high streets
where rain licks the windows clean.

Here where the sea and we wear the glass
smooth and clean and small as rain
on strings round our necks
we have all we need.

—Holly Painter, South Burlington
previously published in *Softblow*, 2015

Evvi and the Butterfly

Under the great, lolling tongue of the ocean;
she keeps her pills: white, shiny and undissolved
like metallic, tiny fish eyes.

Sweet, wilting daisies slip in and out of my dimension
as I wake up again and again but never somatically.

Flashing and mapping and sacrificial capping.

I hold out my arms to grasp all there is
and all there is tumbles past my hands
and into my heart like a hard, glittering stone.

In the spacious, floral air
I pick out specks of light like freckles
and leave kisses, love letters to a temporary home
that is no longer physical.

In my body a garden of painful dearness grows
with every passing layer of ocean
between the beloved and the present.

Whilst dancing I mistook a large, bright butterfly
for the sun
and I could never quite unsee it.

—*Emma Paris, Putney*

In the Inhale

Robins' voices out back
Harmonize with
Piano trills next door
To tell parallel tales of hope
Anticipating, or maybe just acknowledging
Okayness
(Peace feels too bright just yet)

Today, still gray, has none of
Yesterday's bold blue
And clouds puffed with confidence
Its stirring is subtler
Leaf buds, still dormant
Grass, still brown
Wait for a silent cue

We're in the inhale
Before—
I'm always in the inhale
Never the letting go
When momentum carries you
Down and through
Effortless
Or at the very least
Not alone

—Devon Parish, Montpelier

Lost Highway

My entire family is driving to a different state,
A state I don't recall ever setting foot in.
"You'll know it when you see it!" Dad insists.

The sun quickly sinks as we turn onto the highway,
Casting rays of orange and red on the grass.
None of us knew it was this late.

To pass the time, I gaze towards the night sky,
Hoping to spot some familiar landmark.
Nothing ever crosses my vision.

The road lies flat and deserted in front of us.
Never bending,
Never twisting,
Never climbing or falling.

"We'll be there soon! You'll know it when you see it!"
That must be my parents talking,
But they're nowhere to be found.

Pulling the vehicle over,
I shout Mom and Dad's names into the night.
All that comes back is an echo.

—Ben Parker, South Burlington

A Friend Suggests I Get Lost in the Woods as a Way to Find Myself

Today winter hardwoods
stretch like a leotard
over the white skin of the mountains—
lighter on hips, darker in valleys.

I could go there and not get lost,
but probably won't.
Given his suggestion,
what would be the point?

Better to sit here, drink this coffee
bled from Guatemalan hills,
peel another orange to the skin
stretched thin over all that juice.

I'll put it off a little longer—
you know, the Meaning Thing—
like getting lost because
that's how you find Truth.

How many days are like this
when I hold up my arms
and late autumn sun slides down me
like a glove?

Let's face it,
I never chose to get lost at all—
just decided not to panic
when I realized I was.

—*Scudder H. Parker, Middlesex*

Sitting on My Friend's Table

This salmon in front of me
swam long cold miles
in some unknown sea.

Was he netted near the Aleutian Isles?
Did he hatch in a Russian stream,
swim long cold miles

feasting on caddis flies and baby bream
many months after his mother dropped her eggs?
Did he hatch in a Russian stream?

Did he dart between a brown bear's legs,
tumble down the falls,
Many months after his mother dropped her eggs?

Probably, he was farmed in plastic sheet walls
and never had to risk death
no tumble down the falls.

Pulled out, unwilling, like a man's last breath
from some unknown sea
he never had to risk death
this salmon in front of me.

—*Rolf Parker-Houghton, Brattleboro*
previously published in *The Road Not Taken*, Summer 2022

Forward Motion

Often, we ask how many stars are in our sky?
The source of billions of burning suns
With their light reaching across the expanse of time;
Forever glowing in the folds of space
With all the tears of the past to cry
And all of life has really just begun.
Have you heard the precision of the chime;
The melody that you just can't erase?
It blows through you like a violent ocean
As it drowns away the regrets and sorrows
While filling you with an overwhelming peace
And shaking you free of the rattling shackles;
The ones that bind us from forward motion.
It keeps us from productive tomorrows
And a new version of life's lease.
As there are different perceptions to tackle,
We harness the power of our eternal being
While lifting ourselves to a heightened existence.
We must burn away all the dead, useless cells
And bring us into an endless harmony.
The true knowledge begins with seeing
As we give up our petty resistance.
We break free of our destructive, private hells
Using forward motion to be one with eternity.

—*Matthew Patnoe, Craftsbury*

Stored for Winter

In the new cold
under our woolen cover

we fold
together

Two chaise lounges
stored for
winter

—*Melissa Perley, Berlin*

In the Light

I could not paint thee
cause I could not mix the colors so brilliantly
as nature's flowers express your aura

like lilies, dandelions and clover we all look over
seeing your beauty between the grass
    hardly any fragrance until cut down
Your perseverance and prevalence appear

Then tasseled corn with sharp spears
 summer sun bares its bounty with ears to eat
Autumn's trees barren have shed their secrets
 a serenity of blankets below our feet
    few hear them transcending while falling down
    Red, Orange, Yellow that turns Brown
    Dead flowers, snow, dirt and cold

Seasons complete could not begin a pallet
    to describe your beauty
Yet the aroma of all these, in those seasons
Reminds me of how imperfect you and I are—
    But still beautiful!
I could not have seen any of these things
    without your light!

—Edward J. Pomainville III, Rutland

Laments After a Year in the City

The city is ten thousand threads of black
webbing around a single bottled river,

slats of sun slither between the rising,
grimy towers of downtown, afternoons

faded into false light, preemptive dusk,
and we exiles appear to stampede from

bruised and lonely hearts to other hearts
just as bruised and lonely, all of us racing

down those ten thousand black threads.
Here, I might never find what I search for.

—Sean Prentiss, Woodbury

Is Spring an Elegy for Winter?

Remember the quiet monochromatic mornings
brushed with darkness, hushed by snow?

All that patient stillness
interrupted now in the clamor of blossoms

and birdsong piercing my sleep.
This is a loosening, burgeoning time

when lost gestures of the self surge forward
like water over stones.

Softness sustains in memory,
or just beyond it, like my wife's hands

cupping the sides of my face.
But magnolia petals littering the young grass

insist on the brevity
of every delicate thing.

—Alison Prine, Burlington
previously published in *Gay and Lesbian Review*, May-June 2021

oh, darling.

he grazed up under her chin
(using only his fingertips)
gently forcing her eyes to meet his
as he said,
speak pretty little words to me, darling
& all the words just left her head.

—*t.g.prose, Montpelier*

Pop Stars

Pop stars rock
and rocks pop

When we dance
we shake our pants

When we do that
we laugh.

—Saskia Evelyn Kolber Pyatak, age 6, Montpelier

Elms

Each one still green
and graceful as a vased bouquet,
seems a tall miracle,
after all the plague-
consumed skeletons of my childhood,
some cut by my father before they crumbled
and fell from their spots along the wall
above the house, their trunks and branches lit
on some damp fall Saturday.
We would bury potatoes in the coals,
brush away the ashes and eat,
a communion of some sort,
I remember, too,
whenever I see an elm still green.

—*Katherine Quimby, Vermont College of Fine Arts*

Of Fireflies

The summer night they returned
I wasn't inside staring at lights on my many screens.
Instead, I lay in the hammock to escape the house
still stifling from the day's heat. I gazed into the abundant stars
searching the same glowing clusters humans have lost
and found themselves in for centuries: Orion, Cassiopeia, Sirius.

One streaked across my plane of vision too green, too close
to be a shooting star. Then I noticed them one by one
blinking into existence all around me, a magic more intimate
than the heavens. The tiny chemistry sets of their abdomen
mixing a precise solution for bioluminescence.

I lay there surrounded by their mini lanterns
until I wept for the stars distant and dying,
for those spectral beetles disoriented by streetlights and
    fast food signs,
for the people moving too fast to see the short line before them,
and for my heart which beat so slow and sure. In the future
I hope we evolve two hearts against loneliness, the right to
    echo the left
each cooperating to fire its electrical charge on the off beat
    of the other,
lightning flashing back and forth inside us.

—*Kiev Rattee, Manchester*

Geocentric

Looking up at the night sky
I wonder:
what did the powerful priests think
all of those lights were?

When did they realize
the dust of the milky way
was made of suns?

How hard was it,
is it still, to think they had
so under-estimated creation

How embarrassing
their hubris in claiming
our place at the center of it.

No wonder they wanted
to burn astronomy at the stake
and imprison any wondering mind

when the likes of Copernicus and Galileo
dropped that perfect bowl
of priest-guarded heaven
into a glorious, unimaginable sea
of suns.

—Susan Reid, Montpelier

Life

Wake up, do not hibernate
nor keep on slumbering
lift those eyelids from dull awareness
enjoy your heartbeats
life is now, life is here, there, everywhere.

A sachet of wonderment
a museum of memories
life is a tragedy, a mystery, a comedy
a vitality play with you as the main star.

Life is spring when windows open
letting in the blue of the sky
scenting the wind as weeds bow to flowers
one treasured moment after another.

Life, staying childlike, playing, jumping into puddles
walking in the rain, turning frowns into smiles
having no regrets, seeing magic
dreaming of tomorrow's adventures.

Life, a precious jewel, to admire, appreciate,
share, enjoy. So,
love, love, LOVE LIFE

—*vera resnik, Warren*
previously published in *Jo Lee Magazine*, Summer 2022

Inauguration

It snowed all morning as the country changed hands.
The landscape softened, cooled after months and years
of increasing heat. I cried over the baby
sleeping in my arms, and having just eaten,
she closed her eye mid-suckle to rest
without finishing. So much work is unfinished,
and now we task new people with honoring it.
I turn off the television, take the baby to the kitchen,
and run the bath water in the sink.
I dip my elbow in to gage what she can handle
versus what she needs, what will stay warm enough
long enough in the chilly kitchen. When I put her
in the water, she settles, looks up at me in such
complete trust that I am crushed, a garlic clove
in the press. I have to steady myself and believe
I am equal to it, that anyone can be equal
to the times we are in. Here she is with her toes,
the space behind her ears in need of scrubbing,
the folds in her neck and her plump little thighs,
the water she increasingly displaces.
It rises to receive her.

—*Meg Reynolds, Burlington*

The Air Is Made of Glass

The air is made of glass,
 so nothing moves.
All you can do is observe,
 that's the tricky thing, glass is see through.

Nothing moves,
 so you have as long as you'd like to observe.
The tricky thing about glass is it's see through,
 so you don't have to move to see around it.

You have as long as you'd like to observe
 through the glass that surrounds you, transparent
 so you don't have to move to see over it.
What a strange thing to realize.

Through the glass that surrounds you, transparent
 all you can do is observe.
What an odd thing to notice,
The air is made of crystal.

—*Callum Robechek, Montpelier*

Then

Imagination has many voices, memories too;
Ask the amputee, the motherless child
Dreamers who have lost their dream

Ask all that hold guilt in their heart
for all they've done when the red mist rises
Moments of raw rage: truth and anger stripped bone bare

Memories speak most verbose
Tumult, tears and terror, crying out for recognition
like the raised arm of a drowning swimmer
slowly sinking beneath the waves . . .

Our past taunts, a universe of potential
An untapped reservoir of possible
An infinite supply of regret;
memory rewards and punishes
Forgetting is never the answer, though sometimes it's a solution

We dream of tomorrow and reminisce
Without reflection there is no us,
no structure; no tomorrow, no civilization
Memory and imagination are easily confused
Time travels, confusing memory

Life is almost purely past, the before, then
It's all we have, except for that one brief magical moment of now,
all we have is . . . then.

—*Greg Robertson, Northfield*

Memory Silhouette

In the July heat
we'd ride our bicycles to the edge of town
where the roads became gravel
and the sugar beet fields began.
With our BB rifles we'd plink at
doves perched on phone lines,
only scattering tail feathers.

In the January cold
we'd launch our toboggans off the dike
onto the frozen Red River and
cross the state line.
Disheartened by an expected thrill
we'd trudge home in winter's early dusk
wondering where the doves are.

—*Bruce Jefferson Rose, Monkton*

Amphibians

I return from a rapturous adventure feeling freer than before.
Heart solid and set on my new found ascending journey.
Mind open and clear of what's been and ready to see what
    can be.
I feel rambunctious.
I feel ready to face what's to come.
Ready to face destiny.
Baby steps they say.
It's okay to crawl.
So I do.
I crawl my way to the forks in the road ahead making
    carefully thought out choices.
Carefully planned movements so as not to distract the reptiles.
I want to remain hidden.
As not to show anyone my true form.
To everyone else,
I will remain an amphibian.

—Nadia Rose, Montpelier

In Night

for Sue King, and Eric Toy

Guilt stops the opening

of our small houses.

We sweat, we wrestle intruders . . .

We discover angels,

and the Morning Sky . . .

—Scott Norman Rosenthal, Irasburg

Untitled

the stars
deep my heart into
their winding way make
in peals of color
and longing
that to my heart
    (my day-parched heart)
cloy like
fudge and love

—Andrew Ross, Montpelier

Grief is a down comforter and a hot cup of tea.

Grief is not a ghost; grief is a body.
I dress it every morning, and I say,
"What would you like to eat today?"

Perhaps the memory of us laying
in a field, grass itchy, wind warm,
sun-bright eyes closing, soft fur.

Grief sits down at the table, and
sunshine dribbles out of her mouth.

I say, "Would you like another?" and
she nods. She would like another.

So I serve her a gray day on a platter.

Us on the floor, me reading and you farting.
The heater kicking on, clouds pressing down.
The heft of a book, the whisk of a page turning.

Grief would like dessert now. A finale.

So I close my eyes, tremble, and give her
my heart still thrumming with your sigh,
the stiff silk of whiskers, liquid eyes cloudy.

I present with a flourish, a collar, a pile of
dog hair in a bag. I take Grief to my closet.
We sit in the dark, I cry. Grief nods. She is full.

—Jenny Rossi, Winooski

Spirit Days

Penciled lines inside the cover
of my used copy
of Allen Ginsberg's *Indian Journals*
from a woman I've never met

For spirit days of longing
and itchy feet
and on and on
Yes!
Melanie, 1977

The whole book a dialogue—
Allen's street scenes and hashish dreams
Melanie's margin notes:

oh yes,
I remember well
- - -

Oh God, I like this man
- - -

When I was far away in
body, in mind—even now at times
all of "Me Past" comes back
and is "Me in Present" Presence

Ah Melanie, it's been decades
since you inked those lines
from the heart,
a lot's gone down since then.
Allen's been dead for years
and how's it been for you?

Does your heart still pine?
Do your feet still itch on spirit days?

—*Charles Rossiter, Bennington*

How to Write a Poem that is Brief

Pick a topic like describing a leaf.
Don't attempt to write a poem about grief.

Avoid any poems describing a thief.
While you're at it, skip having a motif.

And be sure to stay away from comic relief
or poems about the Great Barrier Reef.

Instead, write a poem about corned beef.
Or else craft a poem about a handkerchief.

And don't dare show your finished piece
to your favorite editor-in-chief.

—*Marjorie Ryerson, Randolph*
from *The Views from Mount Hunger*, 2023

Isolation

My Isolation
Comfort and suffocation
A long cold winter.

—Aaron S., Montpelier

Before the Day Begins

In that small time in the morning
before everyone else is awake,
before the day begins—
with its work and its worries,
its troubles and its stresses.

When it seems that the only ones around
are me and the crow,
who swoops down to eat crusts leftover from last night's pizza.
The sun has just begun to rise—
a golden glow from behind each tree.

The palms of my hands hold my mug of steaming hot coffee
    like bookends.
Only at this hour is my mind allowed to be clear of
    everything else,
with no need to focus on anything
but
the swirling steam rising from my coffee mug,
the early sun shining through the leaves,
and that charmingly-awkward waddle-walk of the crow.

—*Martha Anderson Sanborn, Vergennes*

Directions

Siri!
I'm here.
Driving directions!
Where do you want to go?
Middlebury, Vermont.
Finding directions to Montpelier, Vermont.
No. I said Middlebury!
Finding directions to Montpelier, Vermont.
But I already know how to get to Montpelier.
Are you sure? You've been making a lot of wrong turns lately.
Tell me about it. But that was in Syracuse, and at night.
What about that turn onto a dirt road instead of Route 8 last
    Friday?
Yeah, okay. But I was tired, and it was New York State.
How about in Essex Junction, yesterday?
You're merciless. But I still know my way to Montpelier.
Ya know, you shouldn't be driving at all.
You are a cell phone app—not my mother.
Think of the lives of other drivers you are putting at risk. I
    saw you almost hit that car on Main Street last night.
    Downtown Montpelier, by the way.

Sam?
Sam?
Oh, Siri. I don't know what to do. I'm losing it so fast.
Sam, you are your own best therapist—and your own best
    mother. I can't tell you how to get where you need to go.
    Find your direction.

—Sam Sanders, Montpelier

February 24, 2022

Couldn't face work today so I called in sick.
Now the heady scent of a hyacinth on my table
grounds me to something like Earth.
Dylan croons, wails, whines
prompting tears and adulation.
I work my hands to reclaim my art
and dig deep, deep . . . deeper still
to find the Self I left behind
between jobs and relationships,
mean people and courage.
I'm there somewhere, dancing
"beneath the diamond sky with one hand waving free"
dirt under my nails, paint on my fingers
and Love in the heart on my sleeve.
Russia invaded Ukraine today and I cried
but Koby made a basket on senior night
with a little help from the other team
so there's still hope and I'll keep digging.

—*Nancy Scarcello, Florence*

For Oren, age 4

The branches look like rivers of ink
On a periwinkle field through your window
One more summer, maybe two
And you won't want me
here while you sleep
Snuggled close, cozy in love
The last time I see these trees
will pass unremarked
until years later
when we look back
I hope in unselfish love
I hope in fond remembrance
not weeping for lost time

—*Jeff Seymour, Montpelier*

A Peaceful Winter

Fluffy snow drifts down
Accumulating in trees
Covering the ground

The bear hibernates
The sky is a big blank void
Beautiful soft snow

—Oliver Shoaff, age 11, Montpelier

Flowers and other flowers

Not for the first time
she reckoned the clouds
were bursting just for her

see the way spring swings
in kissing the lilac's tender
branch tips in the snow

not yet not yet not yet

Winter leaves like a bad
taste a lousy guest
littering the last of the

snow in salt and grit
see the way March grips
tight like a frightened child

and yet and yet and yet

April come she will to us
babbling grateful buds
our heads blousy heavy

with sleep and with hope
open to the spell of fragrant
trees, to the possible bees

—*Rebecca Siegel, Thetford Center*

Questionnaire
(for When You See a Mouse in the House)

Are you ready to set the trap for the first time?
Should you use peanut butter or cheese to lure it?
Can you remember to steer clear of the snapping plastic?
Will you be able to sleep without wanting and not wanting to
    hear the crack?
Can you envision carrying this little death sled out to the
    woods?
Didn't you become a vegetarian because you couldn't imagine
    killing something?
Are you thinking about the fly that you slapped with a
    magazine, and it stayed splayed
on the cover but left a tiny splatter of blood on the counter
    that made you think
of a miniature crime scene, and you were the murderer?
Are you regretting not spending more on a Have-a-Heart trap?
Are you wondering if your heart will hurt?
What is tangled inside of you?
Are you imagining that you can share the house with a mouse?
How close is killing a mouse to eating a chicken?
How much death can you get used to?

—*Sarah Dickenson Snyder, White River Junction*

The Old Road

The moon casts light on the gray cold road
In the wet swamp there lays a toad.
We run away from the darkness chasing behind us.
We all feel a sense of security. The light of the moon
 brightens the way.
You can hear the owls say
"Hoo Hoo." He is on a broken down bus.
We come to stop just to see.
We were never running, we were dreaming.
I am Scared. Now it is just me.
All alone I still see the dark road gleaming.

—Sammy Soria, age 11, Roxbury

I Have Been Touched

by the aggrieved
       not by their story of tribulation or tragedy
       not by the abundance of injustice or heartlessness,
       vitriol or violence suffered
No.   I have been touched

by the savage burst of the body and then the mind
    to use that story as a cable
    between that time before the fall
    from a bluff of connection and certitude and
the after the fall filled with empty terror
hazard, loss, ongoing erosion.

Aggrievement lets one still sit and wiggle one's toes over the void
    without knowing existence is always a leased affair
Aggrievement lets one still sense a solid story beneath
Aggrievement is the fast archiving of shock, a mapping of innocence
    an implicit insistence that one is not ready to release the story
    of what life is and where safety resides.

—*Sb Sowbel, Montpelier*

Elysian Time Bump

Ethnophonic po-folks/bumping/bomb-blasting repertoires
of b-flat and conjure/bumping/snake-fingered tempos
into calisthenic wah-wahs/bumping/emancipated jelly rolls
of clarinet and grandeur/bumping/high and mighty high gris-gris
gone crazy/bumping/casting neck-bone elations/bumping/
making elysian spells out of old-born banjos and whole note
    Haitians/bumping/opening windows onto haywire boogaloos/
bumping/clashing voices with the stomping of some heavy storm/
bumping/walking into Birdland in the key of Congo Square/
bumping/feeling mighty fine/bumping/feeling mighty fine/bumping/
feeling mighty fine/bumping/ethnophonic po-folks/bumping/
walking Joplin to the freedom sign/bumping.

—Toussaint St. Negritude, Newark

The Longer You Live in the Woods

The more you feel for what's remote—
the high white clouds filmed by the pond,

the tips of a sapling pinned under heavy snow,
the mouse pelt buffeted by beetles—

The less you buy into the afterlife
The more you trust in resurrection

The closer you stay to the porch
The lower the owls ruffle and swoop

The more inadequate your eyes
The less you meet those of the stars

And at noon venturing under the canopy
the length of a century-old tree

in the silence between chips
you know better than to call songs—news—

made not by a kind of bird but by one you know—
The more they warn you of you

—*Rebecca Starks, Richmond*

The only time I see him

He spills with joy
like the bags of frosting on every counter.
His arm hair, muscles and laugh
too much to be contained
by his apron.

He pours my coffee, bags my loaf
of ciabatta, tucks that little slipper
into brown paper as if he's dressing
a sleeping baby,
hands me our bread child,

leans forward, asks if I've tasted
his eclairs, which I haven't.
Holds one over the glass case
of sugar, *take a bite*, he says
with the pastry at the gate of my lips,

you'll never be the same.

—*Heather Stearns, Wolcott*

I Claim Your Body As My First

I grip your pneumatic hips just up from a low bridge,
collagen curves, like smooth river beds in my hands.
Denim to denim, lip to lip, our bodies heave visible breath,
I am mesmerized, I am entranced, I am moved.
I am compelled, by you, I claim your body as my first.
I want to possess you. I know I will never possess you.
I want to keep you for me alone. I know you cannot be kept.

I want to be your only lover. I know I will not be your only lover.
I want you to want me and me alone. I know you will never
    want me and me alone.
I want to capture you. I know I will never capture you.
I want you to live forever. I know you will not live forever.
This can be said by me. It can also be said by you.
No one can say where first love goes, lost like moonlight over
    a fertile floodplain.

—Bradley Stephenson, Wolcott

Dog and Pony Show

Ennui. Is that the kind of we we are?

The man leading the pony in circles
is worried. Raccoons hide by the hubcaps
of his electric car, his children cry.
My love is neither rustic nor urbane
but suburban, his lineaments exaggerated
by the fat nightly streetlights.

I thought I saw a ceramic pumpkin
on my neighbor's porch, a face punched in
by machine with a light inside
somewhat battery flat, but it was too early
in the season and I was mistaken, we were gathering
apples spilling onto the verge from the lawn
& the manner of creatures crossing
the road was wild in the extreme.

—*Samn Stockwell, Barre*

With Time

Melting icicle
Weeps bit by bit, drip by drip
As with those who mourn

Heartaches day by day
No matter month or season
Accumulation

Eventually
With time the ice just lets go
Likely tears also

—Nancy Stone, Williston

The Red Glove

A glove fell out of her pocket . . .
It lay on the snow red on white,
For a while . . .
It's suddenly taken from its calm,
From the powdered ground,
As strong winds through the woods
Move in and cover the inert thing.

Red disappears,
White dominates,
As it is soon buried.

Soon the snow melts . . .
The glove appears
On top of dry leafs.
It contrasts with the browns,
As it is red and different now.

Many months buried,
Now to be seen,
Refreshed and clean,
It is found by a playful dog . . .
Swished, slobbered, moved,
Broken in pieces, for fun and game.

Left as a nameless fleece,
Scattered on the now dry ground,
Forgotten, not to be found.

—Yvonne Straus, Montpelier

You Tame the Tiger Everyday

You tame the Tiger every day
Blunt his claws so they will stay
Muted for your children's sake
Muted, for your children's sake

You tend the tiger bring him string
The things you do are everything
He is entertained and plays
But you deserve a rest today

His fur you brush
the clothing you wash.
His meat you cut
the meals you make.

He is entertained and plays
but you deserve a rest today

You never know the peace you bring
The things you do you do for them
They won't know until they're grown
All the love that you have shown

You tame the tiger everyday
Blunt your claws so they will stay
Muted for your children's sake
Muted, for your children's sake
But you deserve a rest today
Yes, you deserve a rest today . . .

—*Ashley Anne Strobridge* | *Astrobridge Artistry, Montpelier*

The Mourning After the Blood Moon, Full

I carefully scoop the needles of Pine
from the bird-bath that belonged to my Grandmother

and hold them firm in the palm of my hand, once held by her.
By the waning light of the Full Moon shine,
I bless the needles and place them gently on the pyre.

Rosemary for healing a broken heart,
White Sage to purify the thoughts, and
the last blooms of the Autumn Mums,
to honor my Mother, are added to my flame.

It is a ritual to release the guilt and shame
Placed upon me by the deeds of some few
men, and carried by me like some cross
I was told I must bear.

"Needles of Pine, bathed by the Moon's
shine, I call upon the strength of my
Mothers who are now behind the veil.
Release me from this pain, the guilt and
shame, for the things I have left undone,
for the things I could not have done,
for the things I may never complete."

The Sun rises opposite the Moon, bringing warmth
I cannot yet feel. The Pines snap and
pop like some old bones after standing
too long, still pretending to be strong.

—Karolyn Sudler, Cabot

dAIRY COWs

There's a brown-eyed benevolence watchinG
from the valley, taking the time to chew
things over, dotting the fields
like clusters of stars
pulled north by a
magnetism   my
own cells cannot
fathom, turning
rich and sweet an
abundance I
cannot digest

—*Lynn Parrish Sutton, Burlington*

The Kingfisher

A kingfisher perches atop
a rocking chair down by the pond,
he sits there, regally attired
in his blue-gray and white armor,
surveying his Vermont empire.

On the chair and the ground below,
skeletal remains of crayfish
the king consumed are strewn around
as he holds forth up on his throne,
with the occasional flutter
of wings to pluck yet another
crustacean from the dark waters.

Torrential rain falls, thunderstorms,
yet the royal beast does not leave
his post: drenched but composed, he stays
to thrill us yet another day.

—*Geza Tatrallyay, Barnard*

Persimmon

A trick tomato, you
picked my tongue after
I bit into a homemade scone.

My sister thought you'd cook
out your unripeness—she looked
up later that your tannins

can behead the tips of taste
buds, metaphorically. Now,
your smirk-like skin

flashes on the counter
when I blink. After
feeling nothing at all

for a week, I'm glad your Vitamin
C is still burning in my brain.

—*Alicia Tebeau-Sherry, Colchester*

Oscar Madison

A splotch of tomato red
escapes from the tips
of the clammed linguini
pulled through my lips

It flies through the air
like rocket exhaust
it lands on my shirt
as a bright Papal Cross

Forkfuls run amok
with sloppiness innate
escaping yellow mustard
hits me and not the plate

Without any bib
these stains now display
all time burgers and loaded fries
it's history in a way

Polo, sweat and tee
have marks tougher than Tide
they say you wear your character
so call me eggplant, fried

—*Jimmy Tee, Milton*

The Cello and I

I played the cello for a summer
I lugged it all around
Taking lessons from an expert
I was lucky to have found

We traveled to our weekly class
The big fiddle in the trunk
It wasn't always easy
I kept hoping it had shrunk

Soon I noticed I was rotten
I didn't practice very far
Instead I bought a ticket
To see virtuoso Yo-Yo Ma

I felt bad for my instructor
She really cared a lot
Wanting each and every student
To show talent on the spot

I told her on a Thursday
Our lesson had ended well
But my heart said it was over
Understanding her smile fell

The cello left undaunted
To the rental shop it went
Now I Spotify the masters
Aficionado's time well spent

—Tobe Tomlinson, Essex Junction

Christmas 2020

Choking back tears, driving
Listening to NPR report daily deaths,
Slowing down to look at
A neighbor's dog chained, and tied
To a porch.
There is always something to cry for.
Happiest time of the year,
Looking at pictures of Americans
Choking to death on ventilators,
Merry Christmas and Happy Holidays,
Envisioning maybe next year
We will all celebrate,
Surviving, licking wounds,
Startled and faces drawn, survivors
Bodies touching again, breathing
Into each other,
Hoping to never again wear a mask,
Maybe we will all be more real,
Shuddering off this guilt, rage, regret,
Meanwhile I blur the lines of sadness
And hope,
Letting the lights of Christmas wash over me.

—*Vanessa Tourangeau, Johnson*

I Will

I will dance in the river
I will sing in the rain
I will turn sand into silver
I will shed all my pain

I will spin in the wind
I will grin at the sun
I will Yang to the Yin
'Til my days are all done

I will race through the wheat field
I will fly to the hill top
My fate is clearly sealed
My joy will never stop

All because of you

—*Kathleen D. Towne, Colchester*

Growing up among the woodwork

The synching up of a red line.
Tight from one end to the next.
Brings a laser type noise.
From a pinch, a tug and release.
 Snap.
The chalk wafts into the air.
The cloud coils among itself.
Then begins to settle.
The line lay still against the wood.
It begs for a releasing reveal.
Red finger prints loosen up one end from a nail.
The tension breaks free.
A clearly satisfying crisp line remaining from underneath.
A four foot step dance.
A smile from tooth to hair.

—*Darcie L. Tredwell, MA, Barre*

All Mezclado Up

o

El Amor en los Tiempos de Rage and Fear

o

¿How's your Spanish, Gringo?

"Te Amo" suena mejor que "I love you," pienso yo,
'Cause it's "tu" — "you" — not "I" que leads the show.
En este mundo, que farrago you know,
I look to you as we wait for Godot.
You are my certeza, certainly certeza,
'Midst guerra y tristeza,
sadness and war,
I need you, tan dulce, with such ardour I adore:

¿Serás tú my Valentine, mi amor?

—*Robert Troester, Montpelier*

Laud

Thank you for blue—
azure, cyan, beryl, saxe,
for cornflower dusted with gray,
sapphire tinged with black.

Thank you for boats
with the mercy and strength
to take us across
body after rocking body of water,
our feet not steady,
the deck not still,
but the sky our constant cover—

azure, cyan, beryl, saxe,
star-pierced midnight,
the heavens tucked in tight to a far horizon
waiting unwavering
for our brave arrival home.

—*Betsy Unger, Montpelier*

Wanderers

I tripped over roots in the midnight wood, tripped
out into the clearing and over
the Moon's shadow—
we stumbled in, we tumbled in
the planetary darkness
laughing like drunks rolling
on our backs and we—
rising up to ramble on—
two starlit wanderers—
parted ways again,
old friends

—Deven Valliere, Sharon

Winter Bouquet

Midnight's snow
creates a garden
of fragile flowers
still fresh in frigid air
and windless hours.

Till noontime comes
and with the sun
snow blossoms wilt
to rivulets of water
revealing bent, bare stems.

Yet springtime comes.

—Nancy Vandenburgh, Milton

October Waking

Cold rain pelts the roof
outside our room
where I nest, snug
within sleep's soft down.

Comfort holds as I rise
aware of your presence
two floors below, quiet
in your morning practice

Warmth as I leave the café
hot coffee in hand
ready to be drenched
on a weekend dog walk.

In the end I am soaked
in beauty—leaves
like small red flames
cover the wild shrubs.

Sage colored lichen
climbs the bark of trees
rain darkens branches, trunks.
Streams overflow.

If I had lingered too long
in bed, I might have missed
the mingled joys of a morning
that will never come again.

—Joanne M Vyce, Barre

Family Outing: A Haibun

Mesmerized by the skate park, click-clack of plastic wheels.
Like a flock of birds in low swoops, teenagers zoom the
concrete bowl, hop rails, catch air, avoid crashes. Some
middle school boys in the far end, working a new trick.
One kid falls—no one laughs. *Whoa, Dude!* helps him
up. He tries again—misses the landing. Laughs.

A young dad holds his three-year-old daughter's hand.
Knees crouched, elbows padded, she rolls down a gentle
ramp—comes to a stop, shouts *Yay Me!* with a fist
pump.

> pink helmet
> fierce face
> safe hands

—*Candelin Wahl, Burlington*

You Can See the Prison from the Community College

In winter, when the trees have lost their leaves,
you can see the prison from the community college.
In the classrooms PowerPoints open like crocuses
pushing up through the frozen ground, life experiences
that the class have brought to barter for their education.

You could run a factory on the power of their expectations
when they come that first night after work, the kitchen knife
of second chances at their throats as they run their fingers
along the sharp edges of their unopened text books
praying this won't be the next brick life is throwing at them.

Later in the spring, when they present their papers,
when they come dancing up to the front, stacked heels
and hoop earrings, it won't be any fireside reading,
no moonlight sonata under institutional strip lighting,
more a report from the occupied territory of their lives.

—Simon Walsh, Brattleboro

Not the One

I am not the bat
Striking the ball on high.

I am not the ball
Soaring up into the sky.

I am not the grass
Where cleats rip swaths.

I am not the wall
Where soaring balls strike moths.

In the dim light of the baseball diamond

I am the sky purpling,
The shadow of the lineman.

I am the bruise that's rising
Just at the cheek.

The pain under ribs
The gait, minced and discreet.

—Kim Ward, Montpelier

Whatever Happened to ME?

Nominative, Accusative, such a bother,
such silly conventions to have to learn.

Please, she said, give the book to Bob and I
as the blackboard scratches shatter my brain.
Because, she clearly continued,
me and him are going to read it together.
The chalk and erasers fly through the air.

The careful Germans wouldn't *gib' ich das Buch.*
Surely the fancy French not *donne je le livre,*
and the musical Italians sing *dai il libro a me.*
Me Me Me, I I I, Him Him Him

So please, just hand me the book.
Or maybe give it to I.

—Janet Watton, Randolph Center

Time

Time—in this altered time—
is elastic, not fixed
or mono-directional.
Who says we must
inexorably tread one way,
and that our ages
and experiences
are not layered?
How many find
as they venture a
so-called
one-way track
that five years young
comes closer
with the joy
of eating a cider donut
on the season's last weekend
at a Vermont orchard?
Perhaps time is
shaped like a donut,
and we bend back
on ourselves,
with simple delights
the elixir of our eternal being.

—JC Wayne | *The Poartry Project, Charlotte*

My Beautiful Ghost

I am in possession of a ghost
because I want to be haunted by something beautiful
Omnipresent embodiment of memories
I fear will fade in time

In Life we keep photographs and videos
and messages, emails, texts, notes
because they mark moments
we come back to

In Death they form the body
of what is lost to us
It is a blank sheet
draped, cut, colored with those
paints of the living world
and forming
my beautiful ghost

Please stay with me every day
even as my old brain forgets what is important
I need the definition of the haunting to remain
the clarity of an outline
the features solidified
Substance of something insubstantial
to stop the horror

—T. Wendelken, Montpelier

Migration

Leaving the Great Rift Valley
60,000 years ago
where were you going
no shoes, no map, no road
not even a country to call home
and what did you carry
other than a few words, some tools
migrating through the years
all the way to Tierra del Fuego
passing down your dreams
from two hundred to billions
your penchant for art
iron oxide on cave walls
where you'd rest your head at night
worrying a stone in your hand
not tomorrow
as you drifted off to sleep

—Joan White, Shelburne

Past My Bedtime

I tuck myself in,
 dreading another week at the office.
Then I remember,
 the little plant holder on the side of the street,
 a few blocks away.
It had charming spirals of blue and green beads,
I throw on my jacket over flannel pajamas
 and get into the car.

A few minutes in,
 half the sky's ablaze like a nuclear blast
 or a zillion kaleidoscopes of broken glass shattering.
It's the end of the world, so who cares how late it is.

I drive to the point, the darkest part of the lake
 and there, I hear voices.
Am I dreaming?
A handful of silhouettes who knew all about this:
"It's in the Almanac" they say, *"we've been waiting all summer!"*
And I'm offered a look through a pair of binoculars.
It goes on for a long while,
 as my slippers soak up the cold, cold water.

But what does it matter?
I'm quitting my job!
I'm moving away, far from the city lights,
 just to improve the likelihood of feeling alive.

—S. White, Moscow

I Wonder If

I wonder if the future will be good for me.
I wonder if it will be as bad as I can sometimes see.
I wonder if anyone really does care.
I wonder if people are going to be there.
I wonder if I will ever get paid enough to survive.
I wonder if I will ever thrive.
I wonder if there is a point in getting a degree.
I wonder if there is something great for me to be.
I wonder if life will always be so hard.
I wonder if I will always feel scarred.

—*Cassie Wills, East Montpelier*

Abundance

I am writing for the women
Whose thighs will not be confined
By the airplane aisles and armrests,
By the tight turnstyle of the afternoon train,
By the side seams of slim-cut jeans.

I am writing for the women
Of all shapes:
The apple.
The pear.
The hourglass.
The rectangle.
The inverted triangle.
The pudding-in-a-Ziploc-bag.

I am writing for the women
Who must learn to tend bar
In order to be sent a drink
From an admirer.

I am writing for the women
Whose fiercely fleshy form
Forces folks to
Look, or look away.

I am writing for the women
Whose first words are an apology
But whose last words are "I am worthy."

—Emily A. Wills, Fairfax

In The Trenches, Six Feet Wide

We pull the nib of an apple along the floor.
With my sisters' help, we make it back to the door.
We work as one mighty thorax for our colo—
OW, —ny, I squeak enduring pain from a floorboard

splinter, which hadn't existed before today.
Such is a constant for those in battlefield fray—
trench warfare. Laboring abreast formicidae,
we march onward with our malus trophy now scored.

Our mandibles grow weak from the exhaustion.
We've returned to our waste basket installation—
the base for our army's soldiers and families.
Vainly, we display the half-eaten core. "My liege,

Queen Mother, gaze upon your favorite candy!"
She stares at us disdainfully, her antennae
now raised while nurturing her young. "I am not pleased
with these apples any longer. Go and besiege

another plate of food, my troops! My stomach growls!"
Despondently, the girls and I head out with scowls.
"How will we ever find another prize so sweet?"
asks Antonia, my dear partner. "My love, we will . . ."

I start to say when suddenly a crumb appears.
"Oatmeal raisin! Queen's favorite!" we squeal in cheers.
But soon, we would have to accept utter defeat
as a pair of large fingers snatched up the small spill.

—M. Wilson, Barre

The Coldest December Morning So Far

No wind, no chickadees this early, no dog walkers,
only the motion of the steam rising in the valley
from the city's heat plant, and the slow transit
of the moon sinking toward Camel's Hump.

Suddenly two crows cross from north to south.
The species is getting larger, flourishing
as grassland and shorebirds disappear.

Like cockroaches, crows will adapt, survive
our depredations. Now, the western mountains
are shading orange, the sun is up, the moon
enlarging as it approaches, the way trucks
grew from toy-sized to giants on the flat
Nebraska highway that icy December day.
You almost crashed when a semi slid
across four lanes, pulsed to a tippy stop
in the shoulder gully. Your second-hand
Volvo barely gripped the pavement as you
pumped the brakes. You pulled off at the
next exit, found the college in town,
the student union, begged a group of girls
for a piece of floor in their dorm for the night.

You were 21, on the last leg of a cross-country
trip alone. You are alone again this sunrise
but for the crows, the moon and your memories.

—*Heather Wishik, Montpelier*

What she left behind

Once, when she was here,
I wrote a mem'ry stitched from
Her sister's true words

A silence resounds
Waiting in an empty room
Where does the shine go?

Gone now are my words,
But still, the moon's always full,
Even when it's dark.

—Cat Y., Graniteville

When I was only Peruvian

In the gray city named after a fruit
Gentle shade of brown bodies blooms
waiting in busy corners
greasy smoke from fried sweet potatoes
sticked on their hair, their clothes, their minds

Men calling you or me
Eat! Run!
Jump into my bus!

Crowded minivans acted as buses
Little I knew these people stood with me
Smelling their worries
Worst!
Smiling creeps shading my candor

All kind of men
Big, short, gentle and aggressive
Scaring all girls, Not only me

Rushed to become adaptable women
No matter is in my lemon city
Or in these majestic green mountains
We must!
to forgive all men today

—*Jessica Rocio Robles Yaya, Barre*

To Practice Dying

I never made the request, and yet, my father prays for me. Asks
if I pray? Says his faith has been waiting . . . that it's late. I'm not
sure my faith is that present, is that patient. See, I call the
Farmers' Market my church– every Saturday, I break bread
with Neil, the tall sourdough baker with B.O. I drink the blood
of Yoder, over apple cider vinegar shots, we discuss the
existence of aliens. I pass the basket, sing hymns and praises
to Greg's chickens, for they have the brightest yolks. Offer myself
up to bouquets of kale and feel my spirit lifted, lighter. I imagine
this is what my father, who may not have any more practices left,
seeks. He visited me, just once, at home. I brought him to pray
at my church, on a still day. Sunshine played the tambourine.
Wind licked raw milk gelato. Sweating, he complained, "Too hot."
Kneeled down as if to put palm to palm and put cigarette to sneaker.
We stood on smoke. Close but untouchable. Yesterday, he tells me
He is not afraid of Death—in the same breath that I am his pride and joy.
After all, I am the daughter who doesn't ask of much but sticks around.
He wonders if I would understand a letter he has penned but not sent—
I could question the same, but then reminds me it wasn't until he was
in his forties before he heard a "I love you" from Grandfather
Enoch or otherwise, that he knows trust, that All He has is Truth.

—*Bianca Amira Zanella, Rutland*

did I drop that ball

did I drop that ball
or is it the moon synching through the pines
highway driving steering with my knees
don't worry stop yes I'm watching the road

curious rhythm of light beats on the dashboard
the latest sacred mistake
bouncing there to the west where I dropped it
or is it the moon

will my heart always be this
full of sorrow
can I hope so because
what is sorrow without joy

—*Eva Zimet, Montpelier*

Dilapidated Chimney

Play tri write
rusted tin roof

the yellow siding
Holding black shutters

The Neighbor's chimney is singing
Red

—*Brett, Northfield Falls*

When we come up for air

When we come up for air, Let us be holding each other
... knowing to be tender,
carrying our memories within us
that span oceans,
countrysides, & cities
under gnarly grandmother trees
protecting & cradling us.

When we come up for air, Let all our children be healthy,
fed, loved, and protected
by community, city, & the world
where all our children will be
likened to sequoia seeds
to shade future forests.

When we come up for air, Let our friends still be there
Supporting us as wizened sages
Heartened synapses, & true mirrors
of our souls and visage.

When we come up for air
Let fish nibble our toes,
teach us to prefer simple things:
plants, animals, & rain.

When we come up for air.

—daithí, Montpelier

May I…

    May I live on this piece of land?
If history serves, my life won't be long
I'm not asking to own it, 'cause all land is free
I would like a place to lay my head
To cast off the chains that have bound and sought to
    control me
    Great Granddad never got his forty acres and a mule
He was set loose yet never set free
I'm sure he'd like me to collect the debt that is owed
And I know 'cause I've been told this land ain't free
What I ask for is what is owed by his legacy surviving to me
    May I live on this piece of land?
When the people arrived and put stakes in the ground
Who did they pay for the land that now is not free?
When the people put up fences that contained enslaved
    people that looked a great deal like me
Is that when the land became suddenly not free?
    May I live on this piece of land? Please?
Regardless of where I stray or how far I roam
This piece of land keeps calling me, calling me home
The rivers nearby converge, spring transformation is
    wrought
This land remains not to be sold not to be bought
To be lived on, To be loved on
May I live on this piece of land? Please?

—*Djeli, Brattleboro*
from *The Day After Juneteenth,* 2022

Mama Milk

Mama milk makes me feel good.
It gives me energy.
Mama milk lets me play every day.

—Ezra, age 2, Colchester

I threw some mustard

I threw some mustard at a bird
Because that's the only one that could be heard
No one could hear my parrot colored all lots of reds and
    greens
Maybe because it was sleeping on the epicly epic baked beans
It is sleeping, snoring, sneezing when it woke up then it ate
    the paper with my computer password
Uh oh how will that computer work ever again without that
    word its useless
Wait a minute that's it the word is useless
Wahoo it works yay!

—Jack, Montpelier

To be a cat

To be a cat is to know darkness
To slink and hide and lurk,
To barely know kindness,
To live and breath in murk
To live alone in solitude
To live and hide in alleys dark
To hunt down rats with aptitude
To know the path of the alley cat

The End

—Moana, age 11, Montpelier

The first pillar

The master took us tonight
To the highest point
A bridge supported by two
Gigantic pillars
With a vertiginous view of the valley below
The first pillar
To be realized
Life is suffering
Are you ready to realize this?
The second pillar
The origin
To be abandoned
Are you sharp enough
To see the origin?
My head was spinning
I almost fainted
Partly lost in
Consoling views
from lower points

—*Nitya, Barre*

Schools

Fish

Funny looking they are
In water they are
Seaweed they eat
With gills to breathe.

—Samuel Alvarez, Grade 6
Calais Elementary School

What Time Is It Again?

Yo—its summer lookin kinda dumber sippin some
lemonade sitting underneath the shade getting hotter every
day calendar going June, July, August, September, October,
November and before I knew it I was sittin in the snow and
I didnt even know then I saw a dark crow that was sittin in
the snow then it took off above me and flew back home and
I was sittin all alone when all the snow began to melt and
with singular blink I saw the skating rink became a nice
cool pond then suddenly it occurred to me that it is summer
yet again and that's the end.

—Arawan Azarian, Grade 6
Calais Elementary School

Murderous Eyes

Murderous eyes gleam
Jumping on a roof top hill
Sit atop the world

—Oscar Dean, Grade 5
Calais Elementary School

My Pet Dragon, Who Never Brushes His Teeth

My pet dragon,
His name is Sebastian.
All he eats is fresh raw meat,
And he never brushes his teeth.
His dentist wants to see him,
But it may take a while
Cause' his teeth are pretty wild.
It's almost time
The appointments at nine . . .
But my dragon begins to worry
He feels very hurried.
The dentist comes in
He says, "Show me your grin."
So my dragon smiles.
It may take a while
But he'll use the file . . .
Now my dragon isn't afraid to smile.

—Mae Friesen, Grade 5
Calais Elementary School

Sparkle Puff

S-hiny
P-uffer fish
A-mazing
R-eally cute
K-vell
L-oveable
E-exotic

P-oisioness
U-nique
F-ull of joy
F-un

—*Jillian Larow, Grade 6*
  Calais Elementary School

Thunder

T-errible and scary dark clouds
H-itting the ground with a bang
U-nder the gray clouds
N-early all the animals scramble for cover
D-aringly fast
E-loquently shooting through the sky
R-oaring up high

—Damian Merrill, Grade 6
  Calais Elementary School

California

I've lived there and it's hot
If you think it's wet well it's not a lot
Most days there's a fire
And the temperature gets higher
"It's a vacation." They thought . . .

—Rowan Payne, Grade 5
Calais Elementary School

Lambo

L-oyal
A-lways happy and energetic
M-ellow when he's tired
B-etter than the average cat
O-bedient

—Cole Robbins, Grade 5
Calais Elementary School

A Hundred People

A hundred people went to have lunch
And that is quite a bunch,
They bought a lot of greasy food
Which put them in a *terrible* mood
But that is just a hunch.

—Josephine Taylor, Grade 6
Calais Elementary School

The Weird Apple

The apple ate the marker.
But the orange was darker in color.
The apple happened to die.
So the orange ate a pie.
The pear went to the barber.
After the banana went to the harbor.

—Carson Tetreault, Grade 6,
Calais Elementary School

Marley

Marley is the best dog
Always so cute and fluffy
Rarely a bad dog
Looks like a big teddy bear
Extremely soft and a fluff ball
You would like him if you met him.

—Kennsington Yaehrling, Grade 6
Calais Elementary School

Samantha Jackson's Third and Fourth Grade Class, Calais Elementary School

My Goals

I can reach my goals, I can reach my toes.
Every time I reach my goals I jump up
High into the sky.

I go down low really
Slow, oh gotta go. Oh no I'm really
Low. Now I really need to go.
Back up high so I can fly
So I can see the trees.

The sky is really high.
But I can still fly
Really high.
Oh, bye bye.

—Astrid Andrews-Munson, Grade 3
   Calais Elementary School

Dogs

Dogs can be stinky.
Oh, also dogs can be really cute.
Goofy dogs jump and pull.
Some dogs are silly dogs and do funny things that make
    people laugh!

—*Maddi Bayne, Grade 3*
  Calais Elementary School

Weird Liking

Do you know about the province in QUEBEC, CANADA?
    There's a kid that liked basketball instead of all the others.

—*Silas Blanchard, Grade 3*
  Calais Elementary School

Buzz buzz

I had a friend named Steve and he really liked bees.
    They go buzz buzz and dogs have fuzz fuzz.
It makes me want to run run, and I like the sun sun.

—*Paige Bliss, Grade 3*
Calais Elementary School

Life

As I walked along the ocean shore
I saw above a starry sky
Each one a blazing ball of light
Where aliens might lie

I looked down and saw the dark blue sea
Where fishes swim and play
Where sharks swim and hunt at dusk
And at the break of day

I also saw a field of grass
Where animals play and run
Where field mice hurry through the green
Until the day is done

Animals live in many places
Some where I can't go
Some hunt and play in ground or sea
That's just how things are so

—*Thomas Brown, Grade 4*
  Calais Elementary School

butterfly

Basking in the sun free and flying
Under the shade of the old oak tree
The old butterfly lay resting
The young moth fly away
Every day a new butterfly is born
Right on earth
For you to see
Like a cloud in the sky
Yellow and free a monarch butterfly

—*Kathryn Dodge, Grade 4*
   Calais Elementary School

Stinky Dogs

If you have a dog or two or three do not let them in a bog.
They will stink like a hog.
So if you did, you should have listened to me!
p.s. it will stink up the couch!
p.p.s. you will have to run the cushions through the wash a
    couple times.

—Franny Ehrenfeld, Grade 3
    Calais Elementary School

Bowling

I hear pins falling.
I hear the machines sound like racing.
I hear talking.

I smell ice cream
I smell pizza.

I feel the bowling balls,
they are hard like rocks.
I feel the shoes,
they feel soft and hot.
I feel happy.

I see the arcade
I see other people bowling
I see bowling shoes.
Bowling is my favorite thing.

—Lennox Fricke, Grade 3
  Calais Elementary School

The Bat

There once was a bat. Who wore a hat. But had no friends
so he went to Bat Land. But he only saw Batman. But
finally he found a bat. *Who also wore a hat.*

—Joseph George, Grade 3
  Calais Elementary School

My Friend

Me and my friend like to play here and there.
We like to play together. We like to sit together.
We like to go outside on the slide. We like to swim together.
We want to ride on a horse together.
We like to make snowmen together.

—Ella Grzankowski, Grade 3
  Calais Elementary School

Hockey

I like hockey but my friends always get too cocky

All my hockey equipment always needs drying and my
    mom always knows when I'm lying

—*William Grzankowski, Grade 3*
    Calais Elementary School

The Man and the Cats

There was a man who wore some hats and really liked cats.
One day, some cats came in and they all wore hats.
The man said, "come in." The cats were named Caty,
Laty, and Paty.

—*Colin O'Shaughnessy, Grade 3*
    Calais Elementary School

Monkeys are Funky

Monkeys are funky. But they are funny. But not furry like
a bunny! Monkeys are weird. But they have no beard.
You might be feared! That's okay they don't have a beard
today!

—Elia Jessie Scandale, Grade 3
  Calais Elementary School

Winter

Winter is here. Yay go out in the snow. It's time to play.
In and out the little mice go. It's getting colder.
    It's starting to snow.
No snow is too fluffy. No snow is too wet.
    You'll love the snow I bet.
Tearin' it up outside in the snow. You're on your skis
    or snowboard. Go go go
Entertain with a snowball fight. Hurry up, it's almost
    night because in the winter there is not much light.
Right left swerve a sharp turn. It is snowmachining
    even though you might crash and burn.

—Hannah Singleton, Grade 4
  Calais Elementary School

Cats

Causing mayhem across your house
At every corner there is something broken or out of place
The creatures are catastrophic
Still, you gotta love them!

—*Clara Starr, Grade 4*
  Calais Elementary School

Penguins
a haiku

Penguins are fuzzy
Antarctica is their home
Penguins are all cute

—*Colin Tuller, Grade 4*
  Calais Elementary School

Snakes

Some green snakes
live on branches.
Some green snakes
are different shades.
Most green snakes
are ten inches.
Some green snakes
like to wrap their body
around the branches.
Some green snakes
are scary in the dark.
I like green snakes.

—Andrew Zurowski, Grade 3
  Calais Elementary School

Kiki Adams's Fifth Grade Class,
Main Street Middle School, Montpelier

Summer

Summer
Sweet, healthy,
Warming, relaxing, swimming,
Sunglasses at sea . . . freezing cold
Skiing, shivering, shoveling,
Icy, numbing
Winter

—Adim Benoit, Grade 5
Main Street Middle School

Water

Flowing into different shapes
calming and gentle
Waterfalls rush it into a stream where it
Settles
It cools with the air
Slowly frosting over and going to sleep
It wakes up when the ice melts and the spring Breeze Goes by
and the air starts to get warm
It begins its Journey Slowly flowing in the circle
It starts to rain
The drops gently Landing making tiny ripples Across the water

—*Natalie Flannery, Grade 5*
  Main Street Middle School

Horror anaphora

Here my body lays
Here my body decays
Here my body prays
Here my body daze
Here my body raise
Here my body stays
Here my body craze for my life to end someday

—Camrynn Herdling Julian, Grade 5
  Main Street Middle School

Live Life Freely and Be Who You Truly Are.

Life is sacred . . . be happy that you have it
Life is precious . . . live it wisely
Life is a mystery to be uncovered . . . discover it
Life is an adventure . . . explore it
Life is hard and has struggles . . . be strong and face them
Life is fun . . . so enjoy it
    Life is an opportunity that you should be lucky to have
        been granted for you . . . so love yourself and don't wish
                to be anyone else but YOU!

—Winnie Liu, Grade 5
  Main Street Middle School

Random Things poem

Indeed intruders, tonight would be the true test.
Near the trailer, the place would appear inviting.
As he walked, Come across a cottonmouth moccasin.
That meant he could save his threats.
Though he didn't want a repeat of the fiasco with the
    field rodents.
At strategic locations along the walls of the nuked VCR.
The turkey pot pie wasn't half the cherry strudel,
    surprisingly curly.
Unfortunately the movie was a boulevard.
And one of the co-stars was none other than
    Kimberly Lou Dixon.
A clerk at Blockbuster helped Curly film
    Kimberly Lou Dixon TV commercials.
In the movie, Kimberly Lou played a college cheerleader,
    who got hexed into the star football player

—Matthew Mason, Grade 5
Main Street Middle School

Best Friends

Best friends
If you start to cry
Or maybe shed a single tear your friend will be near.
Best friends
Can make you smile
But you never know how much they mean to you until you
    lose them for a while.

—Maggie McGibney, Grade 5
Main Street Middle School

Opposite.

Liquid,
flow,flexible
soothing,moving,churning,
water,juice..........stone,brick,
staying,building,knocking,
rock,hard,
solid.

—Erik Mohlman, Grade 5
Main Street Middle School

VERMONT
Lush, Green
Rolling, twisting, changing
Mountains, maple syrup, beach, palm trees
Moving, sunning, relaxing
Warm, southern
FLORIDA

—Rocco Nicolet, Grade 5
Main Street Middle School

Beautiful Daylight sky
Raindrops, Kite, clouds, airplanes
Birds, raindrops, Cumulus,
Cirrus, Sharks,
Fish, Sodium, Salt water,
High waters, Deep, cold, Dark Blue
Pretty Night ocean

—Sohfia Ormiston, Grade 5
Main Street Middle School

Here i Stay
Here i Decay
Here i Stay For one more day
Here I Rise to claim my prize
Now the world Must withstand my hand or if they don't
    they will understand

—Maverick Peterson, Grade 5
   Main Street Middle School

Dumb ways to die in Minecraft

Blow yourself up with tnt
Fight a warden with a stick
Get sick with a bee
Invite a creeper inside
Fight a enderdragon with a brick
Jump in the void
Jump in lava
Trap yourself underwater
go to the nether without a sword and shield
fight an evoker with your fist
 jump into the abyss
Clutch with drip stone
Hit yourself with a poison
Look the enderman in the eye and say goodbye

—Nico Plummer-Tripp, Grade 5
   Main Street Middle School

Sticky notes

They vex my day
And Stress me out,
Pressure me
 into over working, writing 13 a day.

They vex my day
When I work hard on writing sticky notes
I can't read,
Pages seem endless words
Then I have to wright about sticky notes 'till my hand falls off

They vex my day
They are the source of my displeasure
Of which I have enough for 1000 men
I come home tired of writing

They vex my day
For I wright 10x more than than I read
I fall asleep
Tired of a busy day.

—Abraham Rosenberg, Grade 5
  Main Street Middle School

One Blizzard Night

The day before
The river flows
The day after
The Sky Snows,
Wind Blows, and the river
A froze.
At my home
A roaring fire.
As I lay down
And begin to tire.
I sleep, and sleep
Without a peep.
Nothing in the house
A stir.
Even my cat—
Only pur.

Although outside,
The world covered
In a blanket of white
The snow storm
A fright.
All one this one blizzard night.

—Monroe J Schwartz, Grade 5
  Main Street Middle School

outer space

Sun
Hot bright
Burning shining swirling
Blossom flame phases untouched
Glimmering,shimmering,glistening
Cold dark
moon

—Owen Smart, Grade 5
Main Street Middle School

Nothing like a cat
Cute in any way
Nothing like a cat
They're really smart
Nothing like a cat
Beautiful like a rose
Nothing like a cat

—Madison Surprise, Grade 5
Main Street Middle School

Northern lights

I watch the sky before my eyes
The colors dance among the obsidian night
A tapestry weaved by the sky above
Swirls of wonder far away
Streaked by blue violet green

—Satya Daisy Tandon-Friedman, Grade 5
  Main Street Middle School

Birds

 birds
Soft feathers on wings
Chickadees so small and light
Fly so silently

—Olivia Terry, Grade 5
  Main Street Middle School

What am i?

Long legs run very fast
Black paws splashing in cool water
Orange fur flows back

—Ellison Zajac, Grade 5
 Main Street Middle School

Windy Kelley's Fifth Grade Class,
Main Street Middle School, Montpelier

Storm

Lightening
I break down trees, I can even snap the powerline.
Yet, people don't fear me as much as they do Thunder.
I *Created* Thunder!
But in the end I get less attention.
I wish I could be Thunder.

Thunder
I can help people sleep sometimes
But everyone is scared of me.
I don't get it. What did I do?
It's so unfair!
People *always* hide from me.
I wish I could be Lightening.

—Ella Andreoletti, Grade 5
  Main Street Middle School

Fish

Slimy scaly
Swimming floating sliping
Fake Real plastic flesh
Gigging Bobbing catching
Sharp pointy
Lure

—Haven Axelrod, Grade 5
Main Street Middle School

TIME: we were young, bright, soulful.
Now we are old but not dark, we are still bright and soulful.
We have hope. some give up. we ….. Survive.

LIFE: I don't understand the way of life.
It can be wrong, it can be right.
 The trees, the dirt, the sun too. all surround me, so do you.

SWEET: love life live long
Beautiful life sweet and long
Respect it and have fun

—Kiersten Briggs Campbell, Grade 5
Main Street Middle School

Rivers

Rivers nice and cool
Cold water takes heat away
Pebbles between toes

—*Molly Campbell, Grade 5*
Main Street Middle School

Roses, covered in thorns
While people weep and mourn
Their hearts black and sore
Black like the love that has turned cold

—*Elena Cannon, Grade 5*
Main Street Middle School

In Spring

Spring comes, sun rises

Flowers bloom until sunset

Tomorrow will come

—Eilidh Corbett, Grade 5
Main Street Middle School

Locklin
Kind, funny,
Shooting, skating, flying
Hockey, goalie ultimate, basketball
Playing, annoying, daring
Kind, funny,
Brody

—Issy Flood, Grade 5
Main Street Middle School

Ocean
Water, Waves
Splashing, Playing, Enjoying
ON   Earth,   Above   Earth
Floating, Orbiting, Flying
Stars, Univers
Space

—*Emmett Hock, Grade 5*
Main Street Middle School

Day and Night

Day—

Bright, Warm

Welcoming, Exiting, Glittering

Sun,   Sky,   Moon,   Star

Terrifying, Blackening, Sparkling

Dark, Endless

—Night

—Madeleine Howard, Grade 5
Main Street Middle School

Painting

The brush keeps dancing

Art is my inspiration

Art creates the world

—Eden Kelly, Grade 5
  Main Street Middle School

Soup

Flow,smooth

Moving,flowing,filling

food   ,weam   ,food, cold

Crunching,bracking,crumbling

crunchy ,hard

Cracker

—Grey Kirtlink, Grade 5
  Main Street Middle School

dead
Cold, bland,
groaning, dying, lying
Mummys, hanging, friendship, color
Breathing, praying, living
Playing, talking,
Alive

—William Moore, Grade 5
Main Street Middle School

—ocean
Wet,   clear
Splashing, playing, freezing
Sea, puddle,   trees, leaves
Living, swaying, breathing
Quiet, peaceful
—forest

—Aedan Nolan, Grade 5
Main Street Middle School

Fans will clap for kickers as i'm sailing through the post and
when i'm caught receivers get to be the ones who boast and
when i'm carried past the goal just look around and see the
cheers are for the running back but why aren't they for me

—Oliver Rivet, Grade 5
Main Street Middle School

Cute
Fluffy, cuddly
Dashing, glistening, calming
Awesome, patient. Bad boi, nasty
Decaying, disgusting, sickening
Sad, troublemaker
Ugly

—Lily Turner, Grade 5
Main Street Middle School

Time

There is not enough time in life.
Not enough time to forgive,
Not enough time to enjoy,
Not enough time to see everyone you love for one last time.
No time at all to make all of the memories in the world.
And not nearly enough time to see the world and everyone
and everything in it.
There is not enough time to do everything you want.
Use it wisely, don't waste it.
You may not have time to live and love before death comes
for you next.

—Lena Vitti, Grade 5
Main Street Middle School

Wendy McGuiggan's Fifth Grade Class,
Main Street Middle School, Montpelier

The cow and the king

There once was a cow
who liked to bow
to me his amazing ruler
Most likely because i am much cooler
But today i am hungry so i guess it's time to chow

—Avram Aguayo, Grade 5
  Main Street Middle School

The only candy I need

Bagged candy for me
Skittles are my therapy
M&Ms are dumb

—Oliver Briere, Grade 5
  Main Street Middle School

Flowers

Many scents.
Many textures.
Many colors.

Ranunculus, as beautiful
As firework finales.

Snapdragons, snapping at
You like an irritated sibling.

Poppies, although they are the
symbol of death, they have
Irrational Beauty.

The ghost orchid, the more
beautiful the more poisonous.

Many Varieties.
Many shapes.

But they all have one thing in common
Inner And outer BEAUTY.

—Ella Mae Coolidge, Grade 5
  Main Street Middle School

Gamer Chad

Yeah, time to lift a bunch.
I am strong jk i like to munch.
Good 81 pounds game all day.
Time to go in my bed there i lay.

—Uriah Croteau, Grade 5
  Main Street Middle School

Candy

        Candy, sweet,sweet candy.
Yellow like the sun, blue like the sea.
        Soft as putty or hard like ice.
    Sniff,sniff a smell so good.
        Candy, sweet for all to eat.

—Nimish Jaliparthi, Grade 5
Main Street Middle School

No such thing as normal

Look on the cover of that magazine
isn't it the prettiest thing you've ever seen?
I want to like her someday
So normal blonde blue eyed
I wanna look normal on the outside.

Hey, see, look.
There's no such thing as normal
Your normal might be different or clumsy
But you were normal even in your onesie

Can't you see
There's a normal for you and a normal for me!

—Eliza Jayn, Grade 5
Main Street Middle School

Vermont

Vermont
     from . . . the snowy peaks to golden valleys
     from, hiking and biking to skiing and riding
     From Newport in the north
      From Stamford in the south
    To the state capital Montpelier to the Queen City of
    Burlington . . . and all the towns in the middle and the
    ridge of
Green Mountains and the Long Trail. That all . . .

—*Jack Lashua, Grade 5*
  Main Street Middle School

A Cry For Help

I wonder, looking at the sea of stars above, can you see me?
    Are you there?
I wonder if you can hear my sorrows, and can you,
    are you, responding?
I wonder, in the vast expansion of the universe,
    who can hear my cries?
There are some things we just cannot know, and yet those
    are the things that we long to know the most.
Such as whether there is someone, anyone, that can see me,
    an insignificant dot in the universe.
So many people in the universe, and none that will respond.
I wonder if you can see me, through the endless wall of space.
I wonder about many things, but many cannot be known.
Despite this, I wonder.

—Dante Muraco and Jack Lashua, Grade 5
Main Street Middle School

Me and Kate

Me and kate are two peas in a pod
Different
        Same
Me and kate
Speaking words to a page
Sun goes down
           Moon comes
   Me and kate
Me   and   kate
Lion mane   bunny fur
Me and kate walking off the page
Moon goes down
          Sun comes up
Me and kate me and kate
Page finish flip the page
Star,sun,moon,cloud
Me and kate
We are so far in we can't see out
All we see is to stars up in the clouds
So we sit out and watch are stars shine out
Because me and kate are just too stars in the sky
      Wondering why

—*Maizy Montalvan-Merrill, Grade 5*
  Main Street Middle School

Me and Maizy

Me and Maizy

Two stars alined
out in the universe out in the sky
Me and Maizy,
Forever lost
but forever found
different colors
different light
Me and Maizy
In the night
our light outshines any two stars in the sky
Surrounded by stars, sun, moon, clouds
Me and Maizy
All around is nothingness going on for eternity life
doesn't seem real like a memory distant and in the
past like i'm slowly forgetting everything someone
hugs me reality comes back still little many years to
go Me and Maizy

—Kate Lucille Newara, Grade 5
Main Street Middle School

Fire Ice

Ice
Cold, Wet
Skating, Sliding, Melting
Snowman, Igloo, Light, Blacksmith
Warming, Cooking, Burning
Hot, Dry
Fire

—Rohullah Rahman, Grade 5
Main Street Middle School

The Beach

I see a girl on the sand
She is from another land
Her towel is bright
It blocks out the light
A water bottle in her hand

—Vanessa Rogers, Grade 5
Main Street Middle School

Spring

Spring is the best time its like you can fly up
In the sky like a dragonfly.

—Remington Russell, Grade 5
Main Street Middle School

The goat that got arrested for holding a saw

The goat I saw has broken the law
Just because he picked up a saw.
why would he do that I don't know
later he threw it into the snow
Soon he got arrested for breaking the law.

That was me, yes I know
I threw my saw into the snow.
I got arrested for throwing a saw. Why?
It's not against the law!
Why I'm a criminal I do not know

—Asia Tang, Grade 5
Main Street Middle School

What am I?

Pink Like Bubblegum
Snorting, Sniffing, And, Smelling
Eating Peoples Scraps

—Lia Tarrant, Grade 5
Main Street Middle School

Frost

Dancing across the window
Sill, drip-dropping
Crying
    Like
        The
    Rain
When
    It
        Gets
    Warm.
The sun is shining with
            A
                 Friendly
                        Grin,
Then it melts away.

—Lula Walker, Grade 5
Main Street Middle School

Students in Grades 2–6,
Roxbury Elementary School

All I am

Nice person
A beautiful girl
Super smart
Infinite strong
Effort into work
Not mean
Illustrates books for fun
Extra nice

—Nasienie Jeshrun, Grade 2
Roxbury Village School

Appetite for Art

Artistic
Daring
Every day I'm hungry
Lives in the forest
Ice cream lover
Never eats broccoli
Excellent at burning myself with a glue gun

—Adeline Keys, Grade 3
  Roxbury Village School

Everything I know

Colorful, I am
Hidden talents
Really great
I love happiness
So I can make a poem
Trees provide us O2
O2 is great
Poop is fertilizer
Happiness is the world
Everything is great
Roxbury is great

—Christopher Legacy, Grade 3
  Roxbury Village School

The best

Best at ice skating
Really good writer
Always silly
Dessert lover
Yellow is my second favorite color

—Brady Moore, Grade 2
   Roxbury Village School

Buzzing Bees

You are a big troop
You are a roaring bundle
You are pretty loud!

—Chance Neun, Grade 4
   Roxbury Village School

Ocean Loving Vermonter

Ocean Lover
Loves drawing
I like ice cream
Vermonter
I despise fish with human teeth
Artist

—*Olivia Oboth, Grade 3*
  Roxbury Village School

Indoors and out

Terrific gamer
A swimmer
Never alone
Never jealous
Eager to go bowling
Really likes sledding

—*Tanner Potwin, Grade 2*
  Roxbury Village School

Why?

Why do i exist?
    Life without any meaning
        The fear of future

—Payton Rich, Grade 4
   Roxbury Village School

Hummingbird

You buzz like a bee
You like sugar water
You're very pretty

—Charlotte Rutter, Grade 4
   Roxbury Village School

School

Everybody is cute and
Very sparkly at school
Eager for snack, and
Recess
Early to school
To read and
To teach

—*Everett Reed Zajac, Grade 2*
  Roxbury Village School

THE KELLOGG-HUBBARD LIBRARY (KHL) is a 501c3 nonprofit that serves as the public library for six communities in central Vermont. KHL has operated continuously as a library since 1895, with only brief interruptions for a polio epidemic in 1917, the Spanish Flu in 1918, the great flood of 1927, the Flood of 1992, and the Covid-19 pandemic of 2020. The Senator Patrick J. Leahy Wing was added in 2001. KHL currently serves the City of Montpelier and the Towns of Berlin, Calais, East Montpelier, Middlesex and Worcester. Learn more at www.kellogghubbard.org.